About the author (and about Jake)

Jake is 9 ¾ years old and lives close to London, with his parents. His favourite sports are cricket, tennis and football. He supports Fulham FC, because his dad forces him to, but he secretly told his godfather Owen that he prefers Manchester United. Jake's greatest sporting achievement is having been selected for the county U10s cricket squad.

Owen is 41 ½ years old and lives in London, but not with his parents. His favourite sports are rugby union, tennis and skiing. He supports Sutton United FC, even though nobody forces him to. Owen's greatest sporting achievement is winning the Collingwood Boys' School Throwing The Cricket Ball competition at the school sports day two years in a row (1982 and 1983).

Owen thinks that Jake is now ready to learn all the sports facts and stories that every man should know……

Notes on Jake's Sports Facts & Stories

Part 1 contains 500 facts and stories, and every fact or story is connected to the one before (but it's not always obvious what connects them).

All the facts and stories are correct as of 31st December 2014.

Facts that will definitely change in future are marked with an asterisk *. For example:

"Between them Celtic FC and Rangers FC have won 99 out of 116 Scottish Championships."*

Facts that may change in future are marked with a double asterisk **. For example,

*"Belgium is the smallest country (by area) to have hosted the Summer Olympics**."*

Facts or stories that are very unlikely to change in future, or which are certain not to change, are not marked at all.

You can use **the index** at the back to find a person, event or story you are interested in.

Part 2 contains 50 quiz questions based on the facts and stories, each of which will require a lot of brain power.

Part 1

1. The laws of badminton state that a shuttlecock must have 16 feathers. Shuttlecocks can be made from either plastic or natural feathers. Natural feathers normally come from ducks or geese, and goose feathers are most commonly taken from the left wing.

2. Badminton derived in the 19th century from the game battledore and shuttlecock, which was played without a net, although variations of the game had existed for a long time. It is not clear exactly when or why the name changed to badminton, but the most widely held assumption is that it was a popular game at the stately home Badminton House in Gloucestershire, which is also the location for the annual Badminton Horse Trials.

3. Volleyball was originally known as mintonette, a name derived from badminton. Mintonette was devised in Massachusetts in 1895 by YMCA employee William G Morgan. A name change to 'volley ball' was suggested shortly after and then in 1952 the name was amended by the United States Volley Ball Association to 'volleyball', although the sport's governing body, Fédération Internationale de Volleyball, is still known as FIVB.

4. In 1891 another YMCA employee in Massachusetts, James Naismith, had already created the sport of basketball to try and keep the young Christian men entertained.

5. In the American National Basketball Association (NBA) a team has 8 seconds to move the ball into their opponent's half (or else they cede possession) and 24 seconds from gaining possession to attempting a shot (or else they cede possession).

6. Jack Nicklaus finished 2nd (or tied 2nd) in more major golf tournaments than he won : 19 times versus 18 wins.

7. Jack Nicklaus is one of 5 golfers who have won all 4 major golf tournaments in their career**, having achieved the feat in 1966. The others are Gene Sarazen (1935), Ben Hogan (1953), Gary Player (1965) and Tiger Woods (2000). Hogan's feat is notable for the fact that he won the only Open Championship in which he played, in 1953 at Carnoustie.

   **Of golfers still playing today, only Phil Mickelson and Rory McIlroy have won 3 of the majors : Mickelson needs the US Open to complete the career grand slam, and McIlroy needs the Masters.*

8. Tiger Woods' real name is Eldrick Woods. Other sportsmen with Christian name nicknames include Jesse Owens (James Cleveland "JC" Owens), Sonny Liston (Charles Liston), and Babe Ruth (George Herman Ruth Jnr).

9. The Boston Red Sox won baseball's 1st ever World Series in 1903, playing as the Boston Americans, and won in 1912, 1915, 1916 and 1918. There was then a gap of 86 years before they won again in 2004. This gap was attributed by fans to the Curse of The Bambino, a reference to the supposed bad luck brought about by the sale of Babe Ruth (also nicknamed 'The Bambino') to the New York Yankees in 1919. On the way to winning in 2004, the Red Sox came from 0-3 down to beat the Yankees 4-3 in the American League Championship series play off, the 1st time any team had achieved such a comeback in Major League Baseball (MLB).

10. After the Chicago White Sox lost the 1919 World Series to Cincinnati Reds and allegations of match fixing resulted in court trials, the team were called the Black Sox. Despite being acquitted in court, 8 players were all disqualified from playing baseball for life.

11. The winner of the Derby in 1844, Running Rein, was disqualified after it was found out that he was actually an illegible 4 year old horse called Maccabeus.

12. The only other Derby winner to have been disqualified was Craganour, in 1913. The race is better known for the suffragette Emily Davison being run down and killed by King George V's horse, Anmer. Craganour was controversially disqualified after a frantic finish involving several horses, and the race was given to 100/1 outsider Aboyeur, one of only 3 100/1 shots to have ever won the Derby. Craganour was owned by the brother of J Bruce Ismay, the highest ranking White Star Line official to survive the sinking of RMS Titanic in 1912, just over a year before the race.

13. 2 American Davis Cup tennis players survived the sinking of the Titanic : Karl Behr and Richard Norris 'Dick' Williams II. Behr's only appearance in the Davis Cup was in 1907, and Williams subsequently played several times, debuting in 1913. After surviving the sinking of RMS Titanic, Williams won the US Championship in 1914 and 1915, and also saw active service in World War One. After the war he continued playing tennis and, as well as playing in the Davis Cup, he won an Olympic gold medal in the Mixed Doubles in Paris in 1924.

14. Richard Williams is the notoriously combustible father of tennis players Venus and Serena Williams. Serena Williams is one of the 17 players (7 men and 10 women) who have achieved career Grand Slams, i.e. have won the singles title at each grand slam tournament at some time in their career** : Don Budge, Rod Laver, Fred Perry, Roy Emerson, Andre Agassi, Roger Federer, Rafael Nadal, Doris Hart, Shirley Fry Irvin, Maureen Connelly, Margaret Court, Billie Jean King, Chris Evert, Martina Navratilova, Steffi Graf, Serena Williams and Maria Sharapova.

    **The only current player who has won 3 of the grand slam tournaments is Novak Djokovic, who has not yet won the French Open.*

15. Only Don Budge, Rod Laver, Maureen Connelly, Margaret Court and Steffi Graf have won the Grand Slam** (all 4 tennis grand slam singles tournaments in the same season). Laver did it twice, as an amateur in 1962 and as a professional in 1969. Graf also achieved the Golden Slam in 1988, when she won the Olympic gold medal in the Women's Singles in addition to each of the other 4 grand slam tournaments that year.

    **Steffi Graf completed the most recent Grand Slam in 1988. Since then, players have come close to the Grand Slam by winning 3 of the year's 4 tournaments on 13 occasions : Novak Djokovic, Rafael Nadal, Serena*

Williams and Martina Hingis (all once), Monica Seles (twice), Roger Federer (3 times) and Steffi Graf (4 times).

16. In tennis, the Open Era refers to the period since 1968, when the 4 grand slam tournaments have been open to professionals as well as amateurs. The last grand slam tournament to be restricted to amateurs was the Australian Open held in January 1968. The French Open, in May/June 1968, was the 1st grand slam tournament to be open and all subsequent grand slam tournaments have been open.

17. In rugby union, the Grand Slam is when 1 team wins all its matches in the Six Nations Championship. The Championship started as the 4 team Home Nations Championship in 1883. It became the Five Nations Championship when France joined in 1910, and reverted back to the 4 team Home Nations Championship in 1932 after France were expelled due to accusations of professionalism in their domestic game. France were eventually readmitted and next played again in 1947, and the tournament became the Six Nations Championship in 2000 when Italy joined.

18. During the Six Nations Championship, the Triple Crown is won by any of the home nations (England, Ireland, Scotland and Wales) that wins all of its matches against

the other home nations. Until 2006 there was no actual trophy, just the name.

19. In US horseracing, the Triple Crown refers to the 3 races the Kentucky Derby, the Preakness Stakes and the Belmont Stakes.

20. In the northern hemisphere, all racehorses' birthdays are considered to be 1st January. In the southern hemisphere it is 1st August.

21. The maximum number of characters a racehorse can have in its name is 18. 'Eighteencharacters' was registered as a name with the North American Jockey Club in 2002. 'Eighteen Characters', having 19 characters, would not have been allowed.

22. In 1991 the last Grand National sponsored by drinks manufacturer Seagram was won by a horse called Seagram. In the following year the race was won by Party Politics, 5 days before John Major was elected Prime Minister in a general election.

23. In 1938 Sir Neville Chamberlain (1856-1944), not to be confused with Prime Minister Neville Chamberlain (1869-1940), claimed that he had invented snooker in 1875.

24. Neville Neville is the father of England footballers Gary and Philip Neville. Morgan Morgan was the father of Welsh snooker player Darren Morgan.

25. Only 4 players from outside the UK have won the World Snooker Championship** : Horace Lindrum (Australia), Cliff Thorburn (Canada), Ken Doherty (Ireland) and Neil Robertson (Australia), each of whom won only once (although Robertson is still playing). Lindrum's victory in 1952 is dubious, as only 2 players took part in the official World Championship after a disagreement between the players and the governing body. Englishman Fred Davis won the alternative tournament held that year, the Professional Matchplay Championship.

    **The highest ranked non-British players are currently Ding Junhui and Neil Robertson.*

26. In golf, match play is a format when players win, lose or halve (i.e. draw) each hole, and the margin of victory by strokes on each hole is not relevant to the overall result. The Volvo World Match Play Championship (on the European tour) and the WGC Accenture Match Play Championship (on the US tour) are the premier match play tournaments in golf**.

27. The Volvo Ocean Race is a round the world yacht race that takes place every 3 years. There is no cash prize for winning the race. It was formerly the Whitbread Round the World Race, and it takes place in stages with

crewed yachts. Other major round the world races include the Velux 5 Oceans Race (single handed, in stages) and the Vendee Globe (singled handed, non-stop). Britain's Ellen MacArthur became the Vendee Globe's youngest competitor in the 2000/01 race when she finished 2nd. In 2004/05 she completed the fastest ever single handed circumnavigation (in just under 71 days). The day after returning it was announced that she would be knighted, being awarded Dame Commander of the Order of the British Empire.

28. All 31 players in the England rugby union 2003 World Cup winning squad were given honours after the victory. Captain Martin Johnson was made a CBE (he was already an OBE), Jonny Wilkinson was made an OBE (he was already an MBE), and the other 29 were all given MBEs. MBE recipients included Simon Shaw, who was brought in as an injury replacement after Danny Grewcock broke his hand, but never played in a game. Coach Clive Woodward was knighted.

29. All the members of England's 2005 Ashes winning cricket team were given honours, with captain Michael Vaughan given an OBE and the remaining 11 players getting an MBE. MBE recipients included Paul Collingwood, whose only appearance was as replacement for the injured Simon Jones for the last test. Collingwood's contribution was to make 17 runs, concede 17 runs for no wickets in 4 overs, and catch out Australia's worst performing batsman of the series, Damien Martyn.

30. Of the British football players, managers or administrators who have been awarded knighthoods in

recognition of their contributions to football, sport or charity, 3 were involved with the 1966 FIFA World Cup victory : Sir Alf Ramsey, Sir Geoff Hurst and Sir Bobby Charlton. The captain, Bobby Moore, received an OBE in 1967.

31. Bobby Moore's full name was Robert Frederick Chelsea Moore. He played for London clubs West Ham United and Fulham but never for Chelsea. Neither Bobby Charlton nor Jack Charlton, Moore's 1966 FIFA World Cup winning teammates, ever played for Charlton Athletic.

32. Footballer Matt Holland did play for Charlton, but never played for the Netherlands (unlike Rinus Israel). Matt Holland did play international football for Ireland, as did Stephen Ireland. Peter Cech has played for, and captained, the Czech Republic. Footballers who played for the wrong teams include Alan Sunderland (Wolverhampton Wanderers, Arsenal and Ipswich Town), Mike England (Wales), Alan Brazil (Scotland), Jason Scotland (Trinidad & Tobago), Edwin Congo (Colombia) and Joe Jordan (Scotland).

33. Timothee Jordan opened the batting for France in the final of the 1900 Paris Olympic Games cricket tournament. Great Britain won the match and are the reigning Olympic champions as this was the only time cricket has been included in the Olympic Games. Only 2 teams entered (Great Britain and France) and Great Britain was made up primarily of a touring side, the Devon and Somerset Wanderers. A quick glance at the French scorecard (including Jordan, Browning, Robinson, Horne, Terry, McAvoy, Anderson and Braid)

casts doubt on their French credentials. The match was increased to 12 a side, and the exact result is a matter of dispute, as the official scorecard does not add up correctly, but Great Britain definitely won.

34. Also at the 1900 Olympic Games, Swiss sailor Helene de Pourtales became the 1st female modern Olympic champion when she won a mixed sailing event. Charlotte Cooper became the 1st individual female modern Olympic champion, winning the Ladies' Singles tennis tournament. Cooper had already won the Ladies' Singles title at Wimbledon 3 times, and won again in 1901 and 1908.

35. The 1908 Olympic Games were supposed to have been held in Rome, but were switched to London after Mount Vesuvius erupted in 1906 and the city of Naples was badly damaged.

36. The 1908 London Olympic Games are officially known as The Games of the 4th Olympiad. London has also hosted the 14th games (in 1948) and the 30th Games (in 2012), even though only 27 Games have been held. This is because the Games that were cancelled due to the 2 World Wars have retained their official numbering : Berlin in 1916; Tokyo, then awarded to Helsinki in 1940; London in 1944). Similarly, the Winter Olympics scheduled for 1940 (Sapporo then awarded to St Moritz then awarded to Garmisch-Partenkirchen) and 1944 (Cortina) retain their numbering even though they did not take place.

37. Only 2 people have won gold medals at both the Summer and Winter Olympic Games**. Swedish figure

skater Gillis Grafstrom won the gold medal when skating was a summer event in 1920 and then, after the sport was moved to the Winter Games, won twice more, in 1924 and 1928. American Eddie Eagan is the only athlete to win gold medals in different disciplines at the Summer and Winter Olympic Games, in boxing in 1920 and in 4 man bob sled in 1932. 3 other athletes have won medals in both games**(Jacob Tullin Tamms in sailing and ski jumping, Christa Luding in cycling and speed skating, and Clara Hughes in cycling and speed skating).

38. The Jamaican bob sled team made their Olympic debut at Calgary in 1988 (where their 4 man team came last and their 2 man team came 30th). Eddie 'The Eagle' Edwards came last in both ski jumping events at the same Olympics. Edwards married Samantha Morton, who is not the actress Samantha Morton that starred with Tom Cruise and Colin Farrell in blockbuster film Minority Report. However actress Rachel Friend, who played Bronwyn Davies in TV show Neighbours between 1988 and 1990, is married to Australian spinner Stuart Macgill.

39. Sri Lankan spinner Muttiah Muralithuran holds the record for the most test wickets taken in test matches (800), followed by Macgill's former Australian teammate Shane Warne (708)**.

*The nearest current player to Muralithuran and Warne (both now retired) is India's Harbhajan Singh, with less than 500 wickets.

40. In 1981, during the last match of a 3 match series between Australia and New Zealand at the Melbourne Cricket Ground, Australian bowler Trevor Chappell bowled an underarm delivery to prevent the final ball being hit for the 6 runs required to win the match. The New Zealand Prime Minister said "it was an act of true cowardice and I consider it appropriate that the Australian team were wearing yellow".

41. The overall leader of the Tour de France wears the yellow jersey. The green jersey is worn by the leader of the points classification; the King of the Mountains wears a white jersey with red dots; and the best young rider wears the white jersey.

42. A guernsey is the sleeveless top worn by an Australian Rules football player.

43. The Melbourne Cricket Ground (known as the MCG or The G) has a capacity of over 100,000 and hosts 4 Australian Rules football teams : Collingwood, Hawthorn, Melbourne and Richmond.

44. The MCG was the main venue for the 1956 Summer Olympic Games, but the equestrian events were held in Stockholm, due to Australia's strict quarantine laws.

45. Equestrianism is one of the 5 disciplines in the modern pentathlon (the other 4 are fencing, shooting, swimming and running). The event is said to have been thought of by the founder of the modern Olympic Games, Baron de Coubertin, who wanted to simulate the efforts of a Napoleonic solider who, stuck behind enemy lines, would have to get to safety using a pistol

and a sword and by riding a horse, swimming and running. Boris Onishchenko was a Ukrainian sportsman who won a team silver medal with the Soviet Union in the 1968 Mexico City Olympic Games modern pentathlon, and individual silver and team gold at the 1972 Munich Olympic Games. In the 1976 Montreal Olympic Games, the Soviet Union finished 4th in the 1st event, equestrianism. In the second event, fencing, Boris Onishchenko was in the epee bout with British captain Jim Fox. After a complaint by the British that Onishchenko's weapon had sounded for a hit despite not having hit anything, Onishchenko's weapon was confiscated. The bout continued and Onishchenko won by a large margin. It was subsequently found that his weapon had been illegally modified so that Onishchenko could trigger the connection to indicate a hit. Onishchenko and the Soviet team were disqualified, and the British team went on to win the gold medal.

46. The suffix 'athlon' derives from the ancient Greek word meaning a contest, and the prefixes bi-, tri-, pent-, hept-, and dec- derive from either the Latin or ancient Greek numbers signifying the number of disciplines. The events listed below are the Olympic events, although there are many unofficial varieties that mix different disciplines and further '-athlons' that have a different total number of disciplines.

Biathlon : Cross country skiing, shooting

Triathlon : Swimming, cycling, running

Pentathlon : Standing long jump, discus, javelin, running, wrestling (stopped being an Olympic event in 1924)

Modern Pentathlon : Shooting, fencing, swimming, horse riding, running

Heptathlon : 100m hurdles, high jump, shot put, 200m, long jump, javelin, 800m

Decathlon : 100m, long jump, shot put, high jump, 400m, 110m hurdles, discus, pole vault, javelin, 1500m

47. The current decathlon world record is 9,039**.

    **The current world record holder is Ashton Eaton, who set the record in June 2012.*

48. Jim Thorpe was a brilliant sportsman who won the pentathlon and decathlon at the 1912 Stockholm Olympic Games, played in the MLB for the New York Giants, the Cincinnati Reds and the Boston Braves and was selected in the National Football League's (NFL) 1920's All Decade Team. At the victory ceremony, the King of Sweden told Thorpe he was "the greatest athlete in the world" to which Thorpe is said to have replied "Thanks, King". He was stripped of his gold medals in 1913 after it was revealed he had received small sums for playing basketball. In 1982 the International Olympic Committee (IOC) reinstated Thorpe's gold medals (but declared the 2nd placed athletes as gold medallists too). Thorpe came top of the Associated Press Top 100 Athletes of the First Half of

the 20th Century, and came 3rd in the Top 100 Athletes of the 20th Century, behind Michael Jordan (2nd) and Babe Ruth (1st). The top woman on the list was at number 9 : Mildred Ella "Babe" Didrickson Zaharias.

49. Babe Zaharias won 2 gold medals (80m hurdles and javelin) and 1 silver medal (high jump) at the 1932 Los Angeles Olympics and once set 5 track and field world records in 1 afternoon. She later won the US Women's Amateur Golf Championship and the British Ladies Amateur Golf Championship, and won the US Women's Open 3 times. In 1938 she competed in the Los Angeles Open, a PGA tour event, becoming the 1st woman to compete in a men's professional tournament – the next woman to do this was Annika Sorenstam at the Bank of America Colonial tournament in 2003.

50. 2 months after Sorenstam missed the cut in that tournament (as Zaharias had done in 1938) the 2003 Open Championship was held at Royal St George's, in Sandwich, Kent. In the novel Goldfinger by Ian Fleming, James Bond plays a round of golf with master criminal Auric Goldfinger at the fictional Royal St Mark's golf course, a thinly disguised version of Royal St George's, where Fleming was a member. For the 1964 film the scenes were filmed at Stoke Park Golf Club in Buckinghamshire, which was much nearer to Pinewood Studios. In both the book and the film, the match is all square after 17 holes, and Bond wins on the 18th after switching Goldfinger's ball, meaning Goldfinger loses the hole (and therefore the match) despite scoring a par 4 to Bond's bogey 5.

51. Royal St George's is one of 9 courses currently on the rota for the Open Championship**. The others are Royal Lytham & St Anne's, Muirfield, the Turnberry Resort, Royal Troon, Royal Liverpool, Royal Birkdale, Carnoustie Golf Links and the Old Course at St Andrews.

52. The Old Course at St Andrews is closed to golfers on Sundays.

53. Eric Liddell was an athlete and Scottish rugby union player, who did not enter his best event, the 100m, at the Paris Olympic Games in 1924 because the heat was to be held on a Sunday, and Liddell was a devout Christian. Liddell trained instead for the 400m, and won. The story is depicted in the 1981 film *Chariots of Fire* which won the Academy Award for the Best Picture.

54. 'Chariots' was the nickname of Martin Offiah, the rugby league and rugby union player. Offiah won rugby league's Man of Steel Award in 1988.

55. The Man of Steel Award is given annually to the best Rugby League player in Britain. Since 2008 it has been voted for by secret ballot of Super League players.

56. In 1975 cricketer David Steele won the BBC Sports Personality of the Year award. Steele won the award after playing in his 1st 3 test matches for England, topping the averages for England in their losing 1975 Ashes campaign with an average of 60.83. He went on to play only 5 more tests, against the West Indies, but is one of only 4 cricketers to have won the Sports

Personality award, along with Jim Laker (46 tests), Ian Botham (102 tests) and Andrew Flintoff (79 tests).

57. The only sportsmen to win the BBC Overseas Sports Personality of the Year award more than once** are Greg Norman (2), Usain Bolt (3), Roger Federer (3) and Muhammad Ali (3).

58. Muhammad Ali defeated Sonny Liston to become World Heavyweight champion for the 1st time in 1964.

59. Sonny Liston is one of 3 sportsmen who appear on the cover of The Beatles' 1967 album *Sgt. Pepper's Lonely Hearts Club Band*. The other 2 were Olympic gold medal winning swimmer and Tarzan actor Johnny Weismuller, and Albert Stubbins, a Liverpool centre forward who between 1946 and 1953 made 159 appearances.

60. 159 is the lowest number above 4 that you can't finish with 3 darts.

61. In darts, to 'diddle for the middle' is when players throw 1 dart each at the bullseye to determine who starts the game.

62. In archery, the centre ring of the target is known as inner gold and is worth 10 points.

63. Lottie Dodd won a silver medal in archery at the 1908 London Olympic Games. She also won the Wimbledon Ladies' Singles tournament when was she was 15 years old (and won the tournament 4 more times), won the

British Ladies Amateur Championship of golf in 1904 and played for England at hockey.

64. It is against the rules of field hockey for a player to hit a shot in a conventionally left handed way (i.e. to use the back of the stick).

65. In polo, players can only hit shots from the right side of the horse.

66. A polo game is divided into chukkas. Each chukka stops after the earlier of 7 minutes 30 seconds or a stoppage that occurs after 7 minutes.

67. A water polo game known as Blood in The Water was played between Hungary and USSR at the 1956 Melbourne Olympic Games. The match took place shortly after the failure of the 1956 Hungarian Revolution. Near the end of the match, Hungarian goalscorer Ervin Zador emerged from the pool with blood pouring from a gash on his face after having been punched. Police cleared the arena, the game was not restarted and was subsequently awarded to Hungary as they had been leading 4-0 at the time.

68. Other famous sporting confrontations include :

The Duel In The Sun : The round of the final pairing at the 1977 Open Championship at Turnberry, played by Tom Watson and Jack Nicklaus. Tom Watson won the tournament by 1 stroke from Nicklaus. On the 16th tee Watson, in the middle of their tussle, is reputed to have commented to Nicklaus "This is what it's all about, isn't it?"

The Rumble in the Jungle : The 1974 boxing match between George Foreman and Muhammad Ali in Kinshasa, Zaire. Ali won, and retained the world heavyweight title, in the 8th round after having spent much of the bout allowing Foreman to punch him repeatedly with ineffective blows that would tire Foreman out (known as 'rope a dope'). Ali then knocked Foreman down, and he was counted out by the referee. A documentary about the bout, *When We Were Kings*, won the Oscar for Best Documentary Feature in 1996.

The Battle of Santiago : The football match between Chile and Italy at the 1962 FIFA World Cup finals. Italy's Ferrini had to be taken from the pitch by police after being sent off, and Italy's David was sent off for kicking another player in the head. Chilean Sanchez then broke Maschio's nose with a punch. When the BBC showed the game, it was introduced by David Coleman as "the most stupid, appalling, disgusting and disgraceful exhibition of football, possibly in the history of the game."

The Battle of the Sexes : The tennis match in 1973 when Billie Jean King beat 55 year old Bobby Riggs 3-0 after Riggs had made disparaging remarks about the standard of womens' tennis. Riggs had played and beaten Margaret Court earlier in the year.

The War on the Shore : The 1991 Ryder Cup held at Kiawah Island in South Carolina. The match became known as the War on the Shore amid accusations on American gamesmanship and jingoism, played in front of an extremely exuberant home crowd. USA won after

Europe's Bernhard Langer missed a putt on the 18th green that would have retained the Cup for Europe.

69. Bernhard Langer was the 1st golfer to be number 1 in the world rankings. The rankings were first issued in 1986 and since then only 16 other golfers have held the number 1 spot**, with Greg Norman and Tiger Woods holding the top spot for a combined total of more than 19 years**.

    Apart from Woods, the only golfers to have been ranked number 1 since January 1st 2000 are Vijay Singh, Lee Westwood, Luke Donald, Martin Kaymer, Rory McIlroy and Adam Scott.

70. Tiger Woods played for the USA in the 2002 Ryder Cup, which took place after the 2001 tournament was delayed due to the September 11th terrorist attacks. The 2 year gap was retained until the next tournament and also thereafter.

71. The 1979 Ryder Cup was the 1st to include mainland Europeans. The USA had won or retained the Cup in each of the previous 10 contests.

72. Since the 1979 tournament, golfers from 7 nations have represented the European team** (in addition to the GB & Ireland) : Belgium, France, Italy, Spain, Denmark, Germany and Sweden.

73. Denmark beat Germany in Sweden to win the UEFA European Championships in 1992, despite initially having failed to qualify for the tournament. Denmark only entered after Yugoslavia were disqualified

(following the outbreak of civil war there in 1991) and as runners up in their qualifying group they replaced Yugoslavia.

74. Dejan Stankovic is the only player who has played for 3 different countries at the FIFA World Cup finals** (Yugoslavia, Serbia & Montenegro, Serbia). Alfredo di Stefano (Argentina, Colombia, Spain) and Laszlo Kubala (Czechoslovakia, Hungary and Spain) have each played for 3 different international teams, although di Stefano's Colombian appearances were in matches not recognised by FIFA. Neither Kubala nor di Stefano ever played in the FIFA World Cup finals, although Kubala eventually made it to the FIFA World Cup finals as coach of Spain in 1978.

75. Spain are one of only 3 countries that have won every FIFA World Cup Final they have appeared in (the others being Uruguay and England)**. 4 countries have lost every final they have appeared in** : Czechoslovakia, Hungary, Sweden and Netherlands.

76. Korfball, invented in the Netherlands in 1902, is a mixed sport with teams consisting of 4 men and 4 women aiming to throw a ball through a basket suspended on top of a 3.5m post. The Netherlands have won 8 of the 1st 9 World Championships, with Belgium the only other winners**.

    **The next Korfball World Championships are scheduled to take place in Belgium in 2015.

77. Belgian cyclist Eddy 'The Cannibal' Merckx won the Tour de France 5 times, a feat matched by Frenchmen

Jacques Anquetil and Bernard Hinault, and Spaniard Miguel Indurain**. American Lance Armstrong won 7 times in a row between 1999 and 2005, although these titles were subsequently stripped from Armstrong because of doping.

***The only current cyclist that has won more than 1 Tour de France is Spain's Alberto Contador (2 wins, and another victory in 2010 subsequently taken from him after he failed a drugs test).*

78. Australian squash player Heather McKay was unbeaten from 1962 until her retirement in 1981. She won 16 consecutive British Opens without conceding a set when this was the most prestigious tournament. McKay also won the only Women's World Championship she played in, the inaugural Championship in 1979.

79. In men's squash, Pakistan's Jahangir Khan was unbeaten between 1981 and 1986, winning 555 consecutive matches including 5 consecutive World Open titles. His run came to an end at the 1986 World Open final, when he lost to Ross Norman from New Zealand.

80. New Zealand rugs are a type of horse blanket made from waxed canvas.

81. New Zealand's men's rugby team is known as the All Blacks, their basketball team as the Tall Blacks, and their cricket team as the Black Caps.

82. Sunderland football fans voted to change their nickname to the Black Cats in 1997. The name was

voted for when the team, known as the Rokermen or the Rokerites, moved from their Roker Park home in 1997. The Black Cats nickname is taken from the nickname of a military gun battery that once stood on the River Wear in Sunderland.

83. There are only 11 clubs in the Football League whose nickname ends in a letter other than 's'* : Portsmouth (Pompey), Middlesbrough (Boro), Crewe Alexandra (Railwaymen), Rochdale (Dale), Scunthorpe (The Iron), Stevenage (Boro), Peterborough (Posh), Leeds United (United), Accrington Stanley (Stanley), York City (The Minstermen), and Fleetwood Town (The Cod Army).

    **Stevenage, Accrington, Portsmouth and York are all in League Two and are therefore the most likely to drop off the list.*

84. The original 12 Football League clubs were : Accrington, Aston Villa, Blackburn Rovers, Bolton Wanderers, Burnley, Derby County, Everton, Notts County, Preston North End, Stoke City, West Bromwich Albion and Wolverhampton Wanderers.

85. Excluding spaces between words and the words 'Football Club' or 'Association Football Club', Wolverhampton Wanderers have the longest name in the Football League. Including spaces between words it is Brighton and Hove Albion**.

    **Watch out for non-league teams Havant and Waterlooville, and Hayes and Yeading United, getting promoted as they have the same number of characters as Brighton.*

86. Bury Football Club have the shortest name**.

   **Watch out for non-league team Hyde getting
   promoted.*

87. Racehorse Red Rum is buried at the finishing line at
   Aintree racecourse. Red Rum is the only horse to have
   won the Grand National 3 times**, doing so in the
   1970s. Red Rum's winning time in 1973 was 9 minutes
   1.9 seconds, a record until 1990 when Mr Frisk won in 8
   minutes 47.8 seconds. Red Rum's time remains the
   second fastest ever despite Esha Ness reaching the
   winning post slightly quicker in 1993. The 1993 race
   was voided as there had been 2 false starts, the 2nd of
   which several riders failed to notice and went on to
   complete the course.

   **No horse still racing today has won 2 Grand
   Nationals.*

88. After Karim Bare of Niger and Farkhod Orupov of
   Tajikistan both false started are were disqualified, Eric
   'The Eel' Moussambani was the only swimmer
   remaining in his heat of the 100m freestyle swimming
   at the Sydney Olympic Games in 2000. The Eel won in a
   time of 1:52.72, more than 50 seconds slower than any
   other athlete recorded in the event. On the plus side he
   set a personal best and an Equatoguinean national
   record. The eventual winner, Pieter van den
   Hoogenband, set a world record of 47.84 in the semi
   finals, a record that stood for 7 ½ years.

89. The longest standing athletics world record is for the
   women's 800m, set by Jarmila Kratochvilova in 1983*.

The next longest standing record is Marita Koch's women's 400m record, set in 1985.

90. In the pole vault, Ukrainian Sergei Bubka was the only man to hold the world record from August 1984 until February 2013 when Renaud Lavillenie broke the record. Bubka won gold in the 1st 6 IAAF World Championships from 1983 to 1997. In the Olympics he did not fare so well:

    1984 Los Angeles : Missed due to Soviet Union boycott

    1988 Seoul : Won Gold medal

    1992 Barcelona : Failed all jumps in the final round

    1996 Atlanta : Did not compete due to injury

    2000 Sydney : Failed all jumps in the qualifying round

91. In women's pole vault, Russia's Yelena Isinbayeva has dominated since 2004 and is the only person to have held the world record since July 2004**.

92. The IAAF does not set a maximum legal length of the pole used in pole vaulting.

93. The IAAF sets the maximum length of a javelin at 2.7m.

94. In 1984 Uwe Hohn threw the javelin 104.80m, breaking the world record by over 5m, in what has become known as 'the eternal world record'. The rules on javelin throwing were changed in 1986 (although the IAAF had already proposed the changes before Hohn's

throw) primarily to reduce the number of flat landings that were difficult to mark but also in recognition that throws were becoming so long that they may become a safety issue. The current world record is 98.48m by Jan Zelezny**.

95. In Mexico City in 1968, Bob Beamon jumped 29 feet 2.5 inches and broke the long jump world record by 1 foot 9.75 inches. Beamon never jumped within 2 feet of this mark. Mexico City is at 2,240m so Beamon was assisted by the thinner air, and the trailing windspeed was 2.0m/second.

96. In athletics races up to and including 200m, and also the long jump and triple jump, the tail wind must not exceed 2.0m/second in order for a world record to be ratified. In the heptahlon and decathlon, the maximum limit for a single event is 4.0m/second and the average across all applicable disciplines cannot exceed 2.0m/s. There are no restrictions on altitude.

97. The Bolivian national football team play their home games at the Estadio Hernando Siles which is at 3,637m. In 2007 FIFA decreed that no international matches could take place above 2,500m because of the adverse medical effects of playing at high altitude, but they reversed this decision in 2008 after much complaint from the South American nations most affected by the decision. The only member of the South American football association, CONMEBOL, not to officially protest against the proposal was Brazil.

98. Although many sources list the football match between Brazil and Uruguay in 1952 as the FIFA World Cup Final,

it was in fact the last scheduled group game as the competition was not a knockout format. The 4 winners of the initial group stage progressed to a final group of 4, and by the time of the final match only Brazil or Uruguay could win and so this match became the de facto final. In fact a draw would have been enough for Brazil to win the tournament, but Uruguay won 2-1 with a goal in 79th minute.

99. Rivaldo, Ronaldo, Socrates, Jairzinho, Romario, Josimar, Aldair are all real names or a close variation on the real names of Brazilian footballers.

100.   Pele, Zico, Kaka, Garrincha, Bebeto, Cafu, Careca, Muller, Tostao and Dunga are all nicknames of Brazilian footballers.

101.   Dunga, which derives from the Portugese for 'Dopey' (a reference to *Snow White and the Seven Dwarves*) was the captain of Brazil when they won the 1994 FIFA World Cup Final, beating Italy on penalties. After their win, the Brazil squad unfurled a banner on the pitch dedicating the victory to racing driver Ayrton Senna who died 2 months earlier.

102.   Ayrton Senna crashed and died during the San Marino Formula One Grand Prix at Imola in May 1994, and is one of only 2 Formula One Drivers World Champions to have suffered a fatal crash**. Austrian Jochen Rindt became Formula One Drivers World Champion in 1970, despite being killed in a crash during a qualifying session for the Italian Grand Prix at Monza. Although there were 4 races left, he still ended with most points and became the only driver to win the

award posthumously. Mike Hawthorn, champion driver in 1958 (a year when 4 drivers died), died in a car crash on the A3 near Guildford just 3 months after winning the title.

103.   Fifty per cent of British Formula One Drivers World Champion surnames start with H** : Lewis Hamilton, Mike Hawthorn, Damon Hill, Graham Hill and James Hunt. The others to have won are Jenson Button, Jim Clark, Nigel Mansell, Jackie Stewart and John Surtees.

104.   John Surtees was also 500cc Motorcycle World Champion 4 times, and is the only man to have won world championships on both 2 and 4 wheels**. Other great multi-talented sportsmen (other than the already-mentioned Lottie Dodd, Babe Zaharias, Eddie Eagan, Jacob Tullin Tamms, Clara Hughes, Christa Luding and Jim Thorpe) include:

C B Fry : Played football for Southampton and Corinthians (including losing an FA Cup Final in 1902 with Southampton); captained England at cricket and still holds the record for most consecutive first class hundreds (6)**; played rugby union for Blackheath and Barbarians; held the world record for the standing jump.

Max Woosnam : Captained Manchester City and England at football; captained the British Davis Cup team and won the gentlemen's doubles at Wimbledon; allegedly once made a maximum 147 break in snooker.

Deion Sanders : The only man to play in both a Superbowl and a World Series**, Sanders won consecutive Superbowls with the San Francisco 49ers and Dallas Cowboys and played 641 MLB games.

Denis Compton : 78 test matches for England at cricket, and 54 appearances for Arsenal FC (including winning the 1950 FA Cup Final against Liverpool).

Jeff Wilson : Played 60 times for the All Blacks, and played 6 one day internationals for the Black Caps.

Eric Liddell : Won gold in the 400m at the 1924 Paris Olympic Games; played 7 matches for Scotland in the Five Nations Championship.

Chris Balderstone : Made over 500 Football League appearances, and played 390 first class games for Yorkshire and Leicestershire and 2 test matches for England.

Rudi van Vuuren : 1st man to play in both the rugby union and cricket World Cups.

105.   Van Vuuren played for Namibia in both the rugby union and cricket World Cups in 2003. In the rugby World Cup he played 1 match (against Romania) but luckily he missed the match against Australia which ended in a 0-142 defeat, still the biggest winning margin in a rugby World Cup match**. He did play against Australia in the cricket World Cup : he was last man out for a golden duck, after having been hit for 28 runs in 1 over by Darren Lehman – this was the most runs scored off 1 over in a cricket World Cup until

Herschelle Gibbs hit 6 sixes off Dan van Bunge in the 2007 World Cup.

106.   Only 4 batsman have ever hit 6 sixes in an over in first class or international cricket**.

Garfield Sobers : for Nottinghamshire versus Glamorgan in the 1968 County Championship, off the bowling of Malcolm Nash. Final score 76 not out.

Ravi Shastri : for Bombay versus Baroda in the 1984 Ranji Trophy, off the bowling of Tilak Raj. Final score 200 not out.

Herschelle Gibbs : for South Africa against Netherlands in the 2007 World Cup, off the bowling of Dan van Bunge. Final score 72.

Yuvraj Singh : for India against England in the 2007 World T20, off the bowling of Stuart Broad. Final score 58.

107.   Gary Sobers held the record for the highest test match score (365), a record that stood for 36 years until Brian Lara scored 375 against England in 1994. Matthew Hayden took the record briefly in 2003, but Lara's score of 400 not out against England in 2004 is still the record**. Lara also holds the record for the highest ever first class score : 501 not out for Warwickshire against Durham in 1994**.

**The next highest test match score in Matthew Hayden's 380 for Australia against Zimbabwe in 2003. The next highest first class score is Hanif Mohammad's

499, in 1959, when Mohammad was run out of penultimate ball of the day when coming back for a second run that would have made him his 500.

108.   A leg of darts requires players to score 501, finishing with a double. There are 3,944 possible ways to score 501 with 9 darts (the quickest possible finish).

109.   A darts score of 26, made up of 20, 5 and 1, is called 'bed and breakfast' after traditional cost of a night's lodging in Britain in olden days (2 shillings and 6 pence).

110.   Phil 'The Power' Taylor is indisputably the most successful darts player of all time, having won 16 World Championships**. The next most successful in terms of World Championships are Eric 'The Crafty Cockney' Bristow and Raymond 'Barney' van Barneveld, both with 5 titles**. Van Barneveld is still playing.

111.   Cricketer Andrew 'Freddie' Flintoff got his nickname from his surname's similarity to cartoon character Fred Flintstone's.

112.   Tennis player Fred Perry won the Table Tennis World Championship in 1926.

113.   Allegedly, during the 1936 Table Tennis World Championships, with the match score at 0-0, Alojzy Ehrlich and Paneth Farkas played a rally that lasted 2 hours and 12 minutes.

114.   The 5th test match between South Africa and England at Durban in 1939 lasted 12 days and is known

as the Timeless Test. Starting on March 3^{rd,} a combination of 2 rest days, 1 day lost to rain, and some huge innings totals during 9 days of play (530, 316, 481, 686), prolonged the match until March 14th. With England in sight of a remarkable victory, rain prevented play after tea on the 10th day of actual play and the game had was abandoned because the England team had to make the evening train for the 1,000 mile journey to Cape Town to catch their boat home.

115.   Len Hutton opened the batting for England in the Timeless Test against South Africa. In 1951 at The Oval, once again opening for England against South Africa, Hutton became the only batsman to ever be given out for obstructing the field in test match cricket**. Hutton top edged a ball, and played at it again to stop it hitting his stumps. Hitting the ball twice to defend the wicket is not in itself illegal, but as Hutton prevented the South African wicket keeper from taking a catch, he was given out obstructing the field.

116.   There are 11 ways a batsman can be dismissed in cricket : bowled, caught, leg before wicket, stumped, run out, hit wicket, hit the ball twice, handled the ball, obstructing the field, timed out and retired-out. If a batsman retires for any reason other than injury, illness or "any other unavoidable reason", and he does not subsequently return (either because he chooses not to or because the opposition captain does not consent to it) he is given retired–out. For the purposes of calculating batting averages retired–out is considered a dismissal, although, like run out, it is not credited to the bowler.

117.   There are only 2 instances of batsman being retired–out in test match cricket**. In the 2001 test match at Colombo between Sri Lanka and Bangladesh, Sri Lanka scored 555 for 5 declared in their 1st innings, with Marvan Attapattu retiring out on 201 and Mahela Jayawardene retiring out on 150. Sri Lanka won by an innings and 37 runs, but there was consolation for Bangladesh as Mohammad Ashraful (playing his debut) became the youngest player to score a test match century. Ashraful was named joint man of the match with Muttiah Muralithuran, and Muralithuran gave his half of the man of the match award to Ashraful.

118.   The man of the match in the Super Bowl is known as the MVP (Most Valuable Player). The quarterback of the winning team has won the MVP award in 26 out of 48 years*, with San Francisco 49ers quarterback Joe Montana the only person to win 3 times (1982, 1985 and 1990)**.

*Tom Brady and Eli Manning are the only current players to have won the MVP award twice.

119.   The term Super Bowl came from a suggestion by Lamar Hunt, the founder of the American Football League (AFL), who had in mind a toy that his children were playing with called Super Ball. The term 'bowl' was already in use to describe post season college football games, deriving from the Pasadena Rose Bowl stadium where the annual Rose Bowl game has been held since 1923. In the 1929 Rose Bowl game, Ray Riegels was playing for the University of California, Berkeley, when he ran 69 yards in the wrong direction, resulting in a 2 point safety for Georgia Institute of

Technology. Georgia won the game 8-7 and Riegels became known as 'Wrong Way' Riegels.

120.   The Rose Bowl has hosted the 1994 FIFA World Cup Final, as well as events in the Los Angeles Olympics in 1932 (track cycling) and 1984 Los Angeles Olympics (football final). The Rose Bowl in Hampshire is the home of Hampshire County Cricket Club, and in 2001 became the 10th British venue to host a test match since the 1st test match in Britain at The Oval in 1880. Lord's Cricket Ground has hosted more test matches than any other ground in the world**.

** The Melbourne Cricket Ground is 2nd in the list, but at almost 20 matches less then Lord's, it is very unlikely to ever overtake Lord's.

121.   Lord's is spelt with an apostrophe.

122.   On the north eastern corner of the Lord's boundary wall, there is a bas relief sculpture of various people playing sport with the inscription 'PLAY UP PLAY UP AND PLAY THE GAME'. The lines are taken from the poem *Vitai Lampada* by Sir Henry Newbold, an extended metaphor in which a future soldier learns about selfless duty in the final stage of a cricket game.

123.   Sachin Tendulkar, the highest run scorer in test match history, never scored a test match century or even a half century at Lord's - his highest score was 37 and his average only 21.66. Remarkably, Tendulkar's teammate Ajit Agarkar did manage a century at Lord's in the 2002 test match (109 not out). Not bad considering that when playing against Australia

between 1999 and 2001, Agarkar scored 7 consecutive ducks, including 4 golden ducks in a row, after which he became known as 'The Bombay Duck'.

124.   A duck is when a batsman is dismissed for nought in cricket. The various types of duck are : diamond duck (dismissed without facing a ball, and also sometimes used to refer to being dismissed on the 1st ball of an innings); golden duck (dismissed 1st ball); silver duck (dismissed second ball); a pair (a duck for the same player in both innings of a 2 innings match); and a king pair (a golden duck for the same player in both innings of a 2 innings match). In the 2nd test between England and Australia at Adelaide in 2010 Australian batsmen achieved the remarkable triple of a diamond duck (Simon Katich), a golden duck (Ricky Ponting) and a king pair (Ryan Harris).

125.   Of the 5 players with the most ducks in test matches**, 4 - Courtney Walsh, Glenn McGrath, Shane Warne, Muttiah Muralithuran - are also 4 of the top 5 test match wicket takers of all time, with Anil Kumble being the other bowler in the top 5 wicket takers**. Playing for India against Pakistan in 1999, Kumble got a duck, and then got 10 wickets in 1 innings, becoming only the 2nd bowler in test matches to get 10 wickets in an innings, after England's Jim Laker in 1956**.

*India's Zaheer Khan is next on the list of duck makers.

The top 5 wicket takers look unlikely to be troubled for a while as the 5th person in the list (Courtney Walsh) is over 100 wickets ahead of Harbhajan Singh and South Africa's Dale Steyn.

126. The Los Angeles Lakers are known as the Lakers because they used to be based in Minneapolis, Minnesota, which is known as The Land of 10,000 Lakes. The Lakers and the Boston Celtics between them have won almost exactly half of the NBA Championships ever held (33 out of 68*).

127. Between them Celtic FC and Rangers FC have won 99 out of 116 Scottish Football Championships*.

128. Celtic were the 1st British team to win the European Cup, in 1967. Since then 5 other British teams have won it or the Champions League** : Manchester United (1968, 1999 and 2008), Liverpool (1977, 1978, 1981, 1984, 2005), Nottingham Forest (1979, 1980), Aston Villa (1982) and Chelsea (2012). Nottingham Forest have won the European Cup more often (twice) than they have won the English Football League (once).

129. Viv Anderson played in both of Nottingham Forest's European Cup victories. In 1978 Anderson had become the 1st black player to represent England in a senior international football match, against Czechoslovakia at Wembley.

130. In the 1940s and 1950's Jackie Robinson became the 1st black baseball player to play in the major leagues since the 1880s. In 1997, in recognition of his career, MLB retired the number 42 shirt from every MLB team – the 1st time a shirt was retired for all teams.

131. Lewis Carroll was fascinated by the number 42 and in Chapter 12 in *Alice's Adventures in Wonderland*

Rule 42 is explained as "All persons more than a mile high to leave the court!" In Chapter 8 of the book Alice is invited to play croquet with the Queen of Hearts. Live flamingos are used as mallets, hedgehogs as balls and the soldiers make the hoops by doubling up and standing on their hands and feet. There is no mention of the peg which players must strike to finish a game of croquet, or whether it conformed to accepted standards.

132.   The peg in croquet is coloured (from top to bottom) blue, red, black and yellow, representing the colour of the balls, then white. Singles is played with the red and yellow, and in doubles the pairs are red and yellow versus black and blue.

133.   A blue is a recognition of sporting achievement given to sportsmen at Oxford and Cambridge Universities. Various criteria apply, and sportsmen can gain full blues or half blues. The 1st University Boat Race was instigated by Charles Wordsworth, nephew of poet William Wordsworth, and it was the second university boat race in 1836 that provided the origin of the blue – one of the Cambridge crew attached some light blue material to their boat, these being the colours of his school, Eton College. In that race, Oxford wore a white and dark blue kit, and subsequently took dark blue as their team colours.

134.   Actor and comedian Hugh Laurie rowed for Cambridge in the 1980 University Boat Race (Cambridge lost). Laurie's father, Ran Laurie, had won an Olympic gold medal in the coxless pairs at the 1948 London Olympic Games. Hugh Laurie went on to win

Golden Globe awards for his performances in TV show *House*.

135.   The house is the area in which the players try to land their granite stone in the game of curling. The stones for all Winter Olympic Games curling have been made by Kays of Scotland who quarry all their granite from Ailsa Craig, a small island off the west coast of Scotland.

136.   Ailsa Craig lies 11 miles off shore, facing Turnberry Resort, one of the golf clubs on the Open Championship rota. The Open Championship has been played on the Ailsa course in 1977, 1986, 1994 and 2009**. In 2009, 59 year old Tom Watson (who had won in 1977) was beaten in a play off by Stewart Cink. In 1994 Nick Price won and in 1986 Greg Norman won.

137.   Greg Norman was married to Chris Evert for less than 18 months. Evert had previously been married to a tennis player (John Lloyd) and a skier (Andy Mill). John Lloyd won 3 grand slam tournaments in mixed doubles (French Open in 1982 and Wimbledon in 1983 and 1984). Lloyd is the only British man since Fred Perry to have won 2 Wimbledon titles**.

**Britons Andy Murray and Jamie Murray, and Jonathan Marray all currently have 1 Wimbledon title to their name.

138.   In the Open Era, Martina Navratilova has won the most grand slam titles overall**. She won 59, more than twice the number that any man has won**.

**Of current players, the closest woman is Serena Williams (33 titles) and the closet man is Bob Bryan (23 titles).

139.   Although various versions of outdoor tennis had existed for many years, Major Walter Clopton Wingfield is usually credited as the inventor of lawn tennis because he published a formal set of rules in 1873 and patented the game in 1874. He patented it as 'Sphairistike', which is an ancient Greek word meaning 'skill at playing with balls'.

140.   The 1st Wimbledon Championships were held in 1877, but the Ladies' Singles inaugural championship did not take place until 1884. In the inaugural final Maud Watson beat her elder sister Lilian Watson. The next all-sisters final was in 2002, when Serena Williams beat Venus Williams.

141.   The last married Wimbledon Ladies' Singles champion was Chris Evert-Lloyd in 1981**.

142.   In cricket, a maiden over is an over in which no runs attributable to the bowler are scored. Byes and leg byes are ignored as they do not count against the bowler.

143.   In horse racing, a maiden is a horse that has never won a race.

144.   In 1993 Julie Krone became the 1st, and so far only, woman to win one of either the US Triple Crown or British Classics races when she won the Belmont Stakes on Colonel Affair**.

145.   Geraldine Rees was the 1st female jockey to complete the Grand National course, in 1982, when she was the last of the finishers. In her other outing in the race, in 1983, she fell at the 1st fence.

146.   Gareth Rees played rugby union for Canada in all of the 1st 4 rugby union World Cup finals. Rees is one of only 16 players to have been sent off in rugby union World Cup finals**. In the match against South Africa in 1995, Rees was sent off along with teammate Rod Snow and South African James Dalton after a mass brawl, the only time 3 players have been sent off in the same World Cup finals match**. As a result of the sendings off, the game became known as the Battle of Boet Erasmus, the stadium in which the game was played.

*The most recent player to be sent off in a World Cup finals match was Wales captain Sam Warburton in the 2011 semi final.

147.   The '99 call' was a signal for the British & Irish Lions to engage in a mass brawl during their tour of South Africa in 1974. JPR Williams summed it up by saying that captain Willie John McBride had told the players "If anybody gets into trouble, you all get involved wherever you are and you all hit the nearest South African to you, the referee can't send off the whole team". The 99 call was used most famously during the Third Test versus South Africa, the original Battle of Boet Erasmus.

148.   Willie John McBride's second row partner in the Battle of Boet Erasmus was Scotland's Gordon Brown.

Brown's opposite number in the match was Johan de Bruyn, who temporarily lost his glass eye during the match. This Gordon Brown is not to be confused with Gordon Brown, United Kingdom Prime Minister from 2007 to 2010. Brown (the politician) lost the sight in his right eye when playing rugby as a schoolboy.

149.   Other monocular sportsmen include:

Jock Wemys : Andrew 'Jock' Wemyss played prop for Scotland in rugby union twice in 1914, before losing an eye in World War One, then playing 5 times afterwards. Allegedly when Wemyss asked for a new jersey in 1920 he was met with a frosty reception and was asked what had happened to the one he had been given in 1914. He was latterly a BBC commentator, whom Bill McClaren considered the doyen of rugby commentators.

Colin Milburn : Played 9 test matches at an average of 46.71 before losing his left eye in a car accident at the age of 28. Milburn was a right handed batsman, so the loss of the left had a huge impact.

Frank McGee : Aged 17 McGee lost the sight in 1 eye after being hit in the eye by the puck playing ice hockey. After a brief retirement, he returned to playing and still holds the record for the most goals scored in a Stanley Cup hockey match** (14 in the 23-2 victory over Dawson City in 1905). He was one of the 11 players inducted into the inaugural Canadian Hockey Hall of Fame in 1945.

Red Pollard : John 'Red' Pollard, the jockey best known for riding Seabiscuit, was blinded in his right eye early in his career, by debris kicked up by another horse during a training ride. It hit his head and led to the loss of sight in his eye.

Mansoor Ali Khan : Mansoor Ali Khan (Nawab of Pataudi) damaged his right eye in a car accident when 20 years old (like Milburn he was right handed, so the impact was less than on Milburn). He played 46 times for India between 1961 and 1975, was captain 40 times, at an average of 34.91. His father was IAK Pataudi who also captained India (and also played for England, most famously during the Bodyline Ashes series).

150.   The England cricket team's tour of Australia in 1932-33 became known as the Bodyline Series, as England frequently employed a tactic of bowling along the line of the batsman's body or down leg side, making it very hard to score. Before the Bodyline series, Donald Bradman's test average was 112.29. During the series it was 56.57. At the end of his career it was 99.94.

151.   The next highest career average by a test match player (completed career) is 60.97 by Graeme Pollock who played for South Africa between 1963 and 1970**. Pollock played against Australia at Port Elizabeth in March 1970, the last test match before South Africa were banned from international cricket. South Africa returned to international cricket against India in Kolkata in November 1991, but their next test match was in April 1992, against the West Indies in Barbados. Despite the 22 year absence, only 10 of the South African team were making their test match debut, as captain Kepler Wessels had already played 24 tests for Australia, becoming the 13th player to play for 2 countries.

152.   The 1st cricketer to play for 2 countries was Billy Midwinter, who played against England in the 1st ever test match in 1877 (and then played 4 test matches for England against Australia in 1881/2). Midwinter took 5 wickets in England's 1st innings, the 1st 'five-for' in test match cricket. Midwinter is player number 31 in the list of England cricketers (and number 10 in the Australian list).

153.   England cricket players wear a number on their shirt just below the crest, representing their order in the chronological list of England players. As the England team for the match against Australia in 1877 fielded first, they have been retrospectively assigned their numbers alphabetically, so T Armitage is number 1.

154.   The Centenary Test Match, played in 1977 between Australia and England to mark the 100th anniversary of the 1st test match, ended with exactly the same result as the 1877 match : an Australian victory by 45 runs.

155.   The 1st ever one day international was also between Australia and England at Melbourne, in January 1971. The 1st batsman to face a delivery in a one day international was Geoffrey Boycott.

156.   Boycotts significantly affected the Olympic Games between 1976 and 1984. In Montreal in 1976, many African countries withdrew in protest at the continued participation of New Zealand after the All Blacks had toured South Africa. In Moscow in 1980, over 60 countries supported an American led boycott in protest at the Soviet Union's invasion of Afghanistan. In

Los Angeles in 1984, most of the Soviet Union's allies joined the Soviet Union led boycott of the games. Australia, Great Britain and Switzerland are the only nations to have sent athletes to every modern Olympic games.

157.   Switzerland's most famous sporting venue is the Cresta Run in St Moritz, used for skeleton racing. Riders go down head first on a toboggan without rakes (on the riders' boots), a way of racing that is different to luge (feet first). Women are not permitted to ride the Cresta Run, with the club's own website stating "Women rode the Cresta Run until the decision was taken by the Membership at the Annual General Meeting in 1929 to ban them from riding, for reasons that are not clear".

158.   Women members were not permitted at the August National Golf Club, host of the Masters Tournament, until 2012, when it admitted former Secretary of State Condoleeza Rice and businesswoman Darla Moore.

159.   The Masters Tournament is often inaccurately referred to as the US Masters. The Open Championship is often inaccurately referred to as the British Open. Wimbledon is, more correctly, the Championships of the All England Lawn Tennis & Croquet Club in Wimbledon.

160.   AFC Wimbledon was formed in 2002 after the relocation of Wimbledon FC to Milton Keynes and their subsequent renaming as Milton Keynes Dons. AFC Wimbledon's 1st competitive goal was scored against Bromley by Glenn Mulcaire, who later gained notoriety

as the private investigator at the centre of the phone hacking scandal that led to the closing of the News of the World newspaper in 2011. AFC Wimbledon were promoted in 03/04, 04/05, 07/08, 08/09 and into the Football League in 10/11. During this period they set a senior football record of 78 league games unbeaten** between February 2003 and December 2004.

161.   Ed Moses did not lose a 400m hurdles race for 9 years, 9 months and 9 days, winning 120 times in a row between August 1977 and June 1987. After retiring from athletics, Moses briefly raced in the USA 2 man bob sled during the World Cup.

162.   In 1964 Great Britain's 2 man bob sled team won the Olympic gold medal. This is 1 of only 10 gold medals that Great Britain have won at the Winter Olympics**, in ice hockey, figure skating (4), bob sled, skeleton bob (2) and curling (2). The 1924 men's curling team were posthumously awarded gold medals in 2006 after the IOC recognised that it had been an official sport rather than a demonstration sport. At the games Sweden beat France in the third place play off.

163.   Sweden beat France in the third place playoff match at the 2011 FIFA Women's World Cup. Having started in 1991, the tournament has been won by USA (twice), Norway, Japan and Germany (twice)**, meaning that Germany are the only country to have won both the men's and women's FIFA World Cup**. The USA's Kristine Lilly has played in 30 World Cup finals matches, 5 more than the men's record holder, Lothar Matthaus.

164.   Matthaus and Mexico's Antonio Carbajal are the only players to have played in 5 tournaments**, although 4 other players' appearances have spanned 5 tournaments** : Elias Figueroa (missed 1974 and 1978 as Chile did not qualify), Hugo Sanchez (missed 1982 and 1990 as Mexico did not qualify), Giuseppe Bergomi (not selected in 1994) and Rigobert Song (missed 2006 as Cameroon did not qualify). Song has the distinction as being one of only 2 players to have been sent off in 2 World Cup finals, the other being Zinedine Zidane**.

165.   Zidane's World Cup history was eventful. In 1998 he was sent off for stamping in his second game, but eventually scored 2 goals in the victorious Final against Brazil. In 2002 injury meant he played only once, in the final group game, as France were eliminated without winning. In 2006 Zidane was suspended for the third group game after picking up 2 yellow cards, before scoring in the round of 16 against Spain, scoring the winner (a penalty) against Portugal in the semi final, and scoring another penalty to give France the lead in the Final before being sent off for headbutting Marco Materazzi. France lost the final on penalties.

166.   Penalties were introduced into British football in 1891. Corinthians FC, founded in 1882, refused to take penalties against their opposition as they saw them as contrary to their ethos of fair play and sportsmanship. C B Fry, a frequent Corinthian, was affronted by the existence of a penalty area : "It is a standing insult to sportsmen to have to play under a rule which assumes that players intend to trip, hack, and push their opponents, and to behave like cads of the most unscrupulous kidney. I say that the lines marking the

penalty area are a disgrace to the playing field of a public school".

167.   Brazilian football team Sport Club Corinthians Paulista were named after Corinthians FC, and have won the Brazilian football league 5 times**. Other football teams with English sounding names include Switzerland's Berner Sport Club Young Boys and Grasshopper Club Zurich, Spain's Athletic Club Bilbao, and Argentina's Racing Club, Newell's Old Boys, River Plate and Boca Juniors.

168.   The derby between Boca Juniors and River Plate is known as El Superclasico. Other imaginatively named derby matches around the world include El Clasico (Barcelona v Real Madrid), O Classico (Benfica v Porto), De Klassieker (Ajax v Feyenoord), and Le Classique (Paris St Germain v Olympique de Marseilles).

169.   The Derby Stakes is also a Classic. The Classics in British horseracing refers to the following 5 flat races : the St Leger (run at Doncaster, first run in 1776), the Oaks (Epsom Downs, 1779), the Derby (Epsom Downs, 1780), the 2000 Guineas (Newmarket, 1809) and 1000 Guineas (Newmarket, 1814).

170.   The most successful jockey in the history of the Derby is Lester Piggott**, who won 9 times between 1954 and 1983. In the 1981 race Piggott and his horse Shotgun was beaten into 4th place behind Shergar (ridden by Walter Swinburn) who won by a record 10 lengths**. Piggott went on to ride Shergar to victory in the horse's next race, the 1981 Irish Derby. In 1983 Shergar was kidnapped from the Ballymany Stud in

Ireland, and neither the identity of the kidnappers nor the fate of the horse have ever been conclusively established.

171. Rene Higuita was a Colombian goalkeeper, who came to prominence with his eccentric displays in the 1990 FIFA World Cup. He missed the 1994 tournament as his opportunities for game time had been curtailed by 7 months spent in prison on kidnapping charges, after he had acted as the go between in a kidnapping case and had received payment (illegally) for services rendered.

172. Other sportsmen who have committed unusual offences include American footballer OJ Simpson (robbery and kidnapping, but definitely not murder), American footballer Michael Vick (dog fighting), athlete Marion Jones (perjury), cricketer Chris Lewis (cocaine smuggling), snooker player Silvino Francisco (cannabis smuggling), footballer Mickey Thomas (counterfeiting and money laundering) and footballer Graham Rix (indecent assault and underage sex).

173. Rix is one of only 8 post-war England footballers with the letter X in their surnames**. The others are Jason Wilcox, Albert Quixall, Alex Oxlade-Chamberlain, Kerry Dixon, Mike Duxbury, Lee Dixon and Graham Le Saux. Graham Le Saux is the most caped X player, and his middle name is Pierre.

174. Pierre Etchebaster was world champion of real tennis for 26 years from 1928 until 1955 when he was 61 years old. Etchebaster was a Basque, and became

champion in 3 main Basque sports – mains nues, pala and chistera – all variations of the sport pelota.

175.   The game showed being played in the credits of 1980s TV show *Miami Vice* is another variation of pelota, called jai alai. Don Johnson, who starred as Sonny Crockett in the show, won the 1988 American Power Boat Association World Cup in the Superboat class.

176.   BBC TV sports presenter Gabby Yorath represented Wales in the 1990 Commonwealth Games in Auckland, coming 8th in the rhythmic gymnastics.

177.   The Commonwealth Games were originally called the British Empire Games in 1930, then in 1954 the British Empire and Commonwealth Games, then in 1970 the British Commonwealth Games, then in 1978 the Commonwealth Games. 71 nations competed in the 2010 Games, but Cornwall did not. The Cornwall Commonwealth Games Association applied to take part in the 2006 games but their application was rejected. In their application, the CCGA cited the precedent of Cornwall taking part in the rugby tournament of the 1908 London Olympic Games, when they lost 32-3 to the only other entrants, Australia.

178.   There are no professional football teams in Cornwall**. The nearest professional team is Plymouth Argyle, less than 5 miles across the border with Devon. Nicknamed the Pilgrims, they are named after the group that sailed from Plymouth to the New World on the Mayflower in 1620 and founded Plymouth Colony

in Massachusetts in the New World. The club badge is predominantly a ship.

179.　　Boston United are also known as the Pilgrims (and their club badge is also a ship). Some different Pilgrims, many of whom were from Boston, England, sailed to the New World and founded the city of Boston in 1630. Pilgrims was a nickname used for the Boston Red Sox in the early years of the 20th century, until in 1908 Red Sox was officially adopted.

180.　　The Red Sox and the Reds (Liverpool FC) are currently both owned by Fenway Sports Group**. Liverpool FC's club anthem is *You'll Never Walk Alone* from the musical *Carousel* by Rodgers and Hammerstein. Rodgers and Hammerstein both won Oscars, (but not for *Carousel*). Only 3 sports films have won Best Picture Oscar** : *Rocky* (1976), *Chariots of Fire* (1981) and *Million Dollar Baby* (2004), a film about a female boxer.

181.　　US ice skater Tonya Harding became a professional female boxer after retiring from skating, recording 3 wins and 3 losses. Harding won the 1991 and 1994 US Figure Skating Championships, but was found guilty in relation to the 1994 attack on fellow US skater Nancy Kerrigan (the winner of the 1993 Championships). Harding received probation, community service and a fine and was stripped of the 1994 title.

182.　　In winning the Ice Dancing gold medal at the 1984 Winter Olympics in Sarajevo, Jane Torvill and Christopher Dean scored 9 maximum 6.0 scores for artistic impression from all judges, the only time ice skaters ever achieved this score (and the scoring system has since been changed). Sarajevo and Oslo are the only 2 capital cities to have hosted the Winter Olympic Games**. Seoul, host of the 1988 Summer Olympics, translates literally as 'capital city'.

183.   Of the 8 finalists in the men's 100m final at the 1988 Seoul Olympic Games…..

1st : Ben Johnson : Disqualified after testing positive for the drug stanazolol. After returning from suspension in 1991, subsequently failed tests for excess testosterone and hydrochlorothiazide.

2nd : Carl Lewis : Admitted to testing positive at the national trials before the 1988 Olympic Games, but claimed it was due to a herbal remedy he had taken, and was allowed to compete.
3rd : Linford Christie : Tested positive for pseudoephedrine at the same Olympic Games but was cleared. Tested positive for nandrolone in 1999 and was banned for 2 years.

4th : Calvin Smith : No drugs offences. "I decided not to do drugs, and lose. I sleep well at night."

5th Dennis Mitchell : Banned by IAAF in 1998 after excessive levels of testosterone were found in his samples.

6th : Robson da Silva : No drugs offences.

7th : Desai Williams : Never tested positive or banned, but linked to George Astaphan who was implicated in Ben Johnson's doping offences.

8th : Ray Stewart : Banned for life in 2010 by the US Anti-Doping Agency after being found guilty of supplying athletes with drugs.

184.   Ray Stewart was a footballer with West Ham United (from 1979-1991) who has an impressive record of 76 successful penalty kicks from 86 taken. The most impressive record** is by Southampton's Matt Le Tissier, who only missed 1 penalty out of 48 taken. Le Tissier was once engaged to actress Emily Symons who played Marilyn Chambers in Australian TV soap opera *Home and Away*.

185.   In 1891 the Football League instructed home teams to have an alternative shirt colour on hand to avoid teams playing in clashing strips (after Wolverhampton Wanderers turned up to play Sunderland in 1890 wearing the same kit). Clubs were required to register their colours from the following season, with a stipulation that no 2 clubs could register similar kits. The second of these rules was subsequently relaxed but the home team continued to be required to change when a clash occurred until 1921 onwards when the away team were required to change.

186.   In the rugby union World Cup Final of 2003 England's inside centre Will Greenwood wore the number 13 shirt, traditionally assigned to the outside centre, for superstitious reasons.

187.   Ivory Coast international footballer Kolo Toure's superstition is to always be the last of his team on to the pitch. When playing for Arsenal against Roma in 2009, he was late out for the second half as he was waiting for William Gallas (who was having extended treatment on an injury) before coming on. As the second half had already started, Toure was booked for entering the field of play without permission.

188.   One of the superstitions of Wade Boggs, a baseball player who won the World Series with the New York Yankees in 1996, was to eat chicken before every game.

189.   The Champions Dinner takes place on the Tuesday before the Masters Tournament starts, and all previous winners welcome the defending Champion, who selects (and pays for) the menu. 4 time winner Tiger Woods' menu has involved chicken in each of his selections**. Players often choose nationality themed dishes : Nick Faldo chose fish and chips in 1997, Jose Maria Olazabal chose paella in 1995, Sandy Lyle chose haggis, neeps and tatties in 1989, and Bernhard Langer chose Wiener schnitzel in 1986.

190.   Every year since 1960, on the Wednesday before the Masters Tournament starts, the players hold a contest over the 1,060 yard 9 hole par 3 course. No winner of the par 3 contest has ever won the Masters in the same year**. Luke Donald became the 1st Englishmen to win the par 3 contest in 2011.

191.   Donald's full name is Luke Campbell Donald. Donald Campbell broke 8 world speed records in the

1950s and 1960s, and his father Sir Malcolm Campbell has held both records at various times.

192.   Other sons who emulated their sons in the same sports include :

Ian and Liam Botham : Ian Botham is one of England's greatest ever cricket all-rounders, finishing his career with a test match batting average of 33.54 and a bowling average of 38.40, and having captained England 12 times. Botham also played in the Football League for Scunthorpe United. Son Liam played for Hampshire, taking the wicket of ex-England captain Mike Gatting on his debut, before switching to rugby union, and later rugby league.

Chris and Stuart Broad : Father Chris played 25 test matches and 34 one day internationals as a batsman for England. Son Stuart is a bowler who has captained the T20 England team.

Andy and Owen Farrell : Father Andy won rugby league's Man of Steel award 3 times and played 45 times for England and Great Britain, and 8 times for England at rugby union. Son Owen has played for England's rugby union team.

Gilles and Jacques Villeneuve : Both Formula One drivers, Gilles raced for Ferrari from 1977-1982, winning 6 Grand Prix and achieving a career best 2nd place in 1979, and son Jacques won the title in 1997. **Graham and Damon Hill** : The only father and son to have both become Formula One World Drivers Champion**.

Bobby and Barry Bonds : In baseball, Barry was a National League MVP a record 7 times, and father Bobby played in the All Star game 3 times.**Colin and**

Chris Cowdrey : The only father and son to have both captained the England cricket team.**

193.   Chris Cowdrey was one of 4 players to captain England in the 5 match 1988 test match series against the West Indies (the others were Mike Gatting, John Emburey and Graham Gooch). England's Chairman of Selectors at the time was Peter May who was Cowdrey's godfather : before being made captain, Cowdrey's test batting average was 19.20 and his bowling average was 72.00. England lost the match by 10 wickets and Cowdrey never played for England again.

194.   Cowdray Park in West Sussex is the UK's leading polo venue. It hosts the UK's premier annual polo tournament, the Gold Cup.

195.   Other Gold Cups include the Cheltenham Gold Cup (the most valuable non-handicap national hunt race in Britain), the CONCACAF Gold Cup (biennial football tournament for North American, Central American and Caribbean football teams) and the American Power Boat Association Gold Cup.

196.   The oldest active trophy in international sport is the America's Cup. The race is named after America, the yacht that in 1851 won the annual Royal Yacht Squadron's annual race around the Isle of Wight and

then dedicated the cup to the New York Yacht Club to be a perpetual yachting challenge between nations.

197.   In 1995 the Cup was won by the Royal New Zealand Yacht Squadron's NZL32, nicknamed Black Magic. In 1997 the Squadron's clubhouse was broken into and the Cup damaged in a political protest by a Maori called Penehamine Pere Netana-Patuawa.

198.   Duke Paoa Kahinu Makoe Hulikohua Kahanamoku was partly responsible for the theft of the 1st Olympic Flag, which had been presented to the IOC at the 1920 Antwerp Olympic Games, but could not be found at the end of the Games. In 1997, at a banquet hosted by the US Olympic Committee in Philadelphia, a reporter was interviewing Hal Haig Prieste who had won a bronze medal in platform diving as a member of the 1920 US Olympic team. The reporter mentioned that the IOC had not been able to find out what had happened to the original Olympic flag. "I can help you with that," Prieste said, "It's home in my suitcase." At the end of the Games, spurred on by teammate and gold medal winning swimmer Duke Kahanamoku, he shimmied up a flagpole and stole the Olympic Flag, despite being chased by some policemen. For 77 years the flag was stored away in the bottom of his suitcase. The flag was returned to the IOC by Prieste, by then 103 years old and the oldest living Olympian, in a special ceremony held at the 2000 Olympic Games in Sydney. The Antwerp Flag is now on display at the Olympic Museum in Lausanne, Switzerland, with a plaque thanking Prieste for donating it.

199.   The Jules Rimet Trophy was stolen in England in March 1966 but found under a hedge in South Norwood, London (less than 2 miles from Crystal Palace FC's ground) by Pickles the dog only a week later.

200.   The last time England conceded the 1st goal in a World Cup finals match and came back to win the match was the World Cup Final of 1966**.

201.   England's right back in the 1966 final, George Cohen, is the uncle of Ben Cohen who won the 2003 rugby union World Cup with England.

202.   The origins of rugby are obscure, but the most popular story is that in 1823 William Webb Ellis, a pupil at Rugby School, caught the ball during a game of football and ran with it. The plaque at the school reads "This stone commemorates the exploit of William Webb Ellis who with a fine disregard for the rules of football as played in his time first took the ball in his arms and ran with it thus originating the distinctive feature of the rugby game AD 1823".

203.   A hand, used to measure the height of horses, is equal to 4 inches.

204.   Diego Maradona scored the Hand of God goal against England in the quarter final of the 1986 FIFA World Cup, when he punched the ball past Peter Shilton, but Tunisian referee Ali Bin Nasser failed to spot the obvious handball. 5 other shocking World Cup refereeing decisions include:

France vs Kuwait 1982 : After France went 4-1 up in a group game, Sheikh Fahad Al-Ahmad Al-Sabah, president of the Kuwait Football Association, took the Kuwaiti players off the pitch, insisting that they had heard the referee whistle to stop play. He accosted referee Miroslav Stupar, who gave in and disallowed the goal. Maxim Bossis added a 4th in the 89th minute anyway to make it 4-1 again.

Brazil vs Sweden 1978 : In the group game in 1978, referee Clive Thomas blew for full time after a corner had been taken, but before it has been headed directly into the net less than 1 second later. This prevented a Brazil victory, which impacted group placings and potential future opponents.

Croatia vs Australia 2006 : In a group game in 2006, referee Graham Poll booked Croatia's Josip Simunic after 61 minutes, after 90 minutes and then for a third time as the players were walking off, finally remembering to show him a red card. The FIFA official match report only lists 2 yellow cards, but Poll has gone on record to say that he made a mistake and issued 3 yellow cards, and was just relieved that Simunic didn't score a goal after not being sent off.

Australia vs Equatorial Guinea 2011 : In the FIFA Women's World Cup, Equatorial Guinea's Bruna caught the ball in both hands after it rebounded off the post, holding on to it (and looking a bit confused) in full view for over a second, before dropping it and casually running off. Hungarian referee Gyoengyi Gaal somehow decided this was not a penalty, but Australia won anyway.

West Germany vs France 1982 : In the semi final in 1982, with the score 1-1 after 60 minutes, Patrick Battiston raced on to a through ball from Michael Platini and poked it past the onrushing German goalkeeper Harald Schumacher. Schumacher hit Battiston in mid air, the ball rolled wide of the post, and Battiston lay unconscious on the turf with damaged vertebrae and missing teeth, later slipping into a coma. Dutch referee Charles Corver gave a goal kick. West Germany went on to win on penalties.

205. Germany's Michael Schumacher won 91 Formula One Grand Prix in his career. His brother Ralf won 6 Grand Prix and they are the only brothers to have both won Grand Prix**.

206. American jockey Willie Shoemaker held the world record for the most professional victories for 29 years, ending with 8,833 wins. The current record holder, Russell Baze, has over over 12,000 wins and is still racing**.

207. The Cobblers is the nickname of Northampton Town FC, who are one of only 5 English league teams whose names start and end in the same letter, the others being Liverpool, Aston Villa, Charlton Athletic and York City. In Scotland there are 5 : Celtic, Kilmarnock, East Fife, East Stirlingshire and Dundee United**.

208. Dundee is one of only 9 cities that have supplied more than 1 European Cup/Champions League semi finalist**. The other cities are Madrid, Milan, London,

Belgrade, Glasgow, Bucharest, Vienna and Prague (Sparta Prague and Dukla Prague).

209.   The song All I Want For Christmas Is A Dukla Prague Away Kit is a song by British pop group Half Man Half Biscuit. Other footballing references in the group's lyrics include presenters/commentators Brian Moore, Dickie Davies, Jim Beglin, Tony Gubba, Elton Welsby, Bob Wilson, Kenneth Wolstenholme and Jim Rosenthal, goalkeepers Lev Yashin, Mart Poom and Brad Freidel, players Ferenc Puskas, Nobby Stiles, Bobby Charlton, Zinedine Zidane, Zico, Gianfranco Zola, Antonio Zubizaretta, Dino Zoff, Romeo Zondervan, Barry Venison, Alan Brazil and Neil Ruddock, and clubs Honved, Chelsea, Accrington Stanley, Barcelona, Borussia Monchengladbach and Farnborough Town. Other sporting references in the group's songs include korfball, tennis players Virginia Wade and Vitas Gerulaitis, and 1983 World Champion Finnish rally driver Hannu Mikkola.

210.   Mikkola's 1st rally was the 1973 Monte Carlo rally. Mikkola never won the Monte Carlo rally (2nd twice, 3rd twice). The winner of the race in 1953 was Dutch rally driver Maus Gatsonides. Gatsonides is more famous for inventing the Gatso speed camera in use by many police forces. He originally developed the device in order to measure his cornering speed.

211.   In 1998, the 1992 Formula One World Drivers Champion Nigel Mansell was banned from driving for 6 months after being caught speeding – at the time he was a Special Constable for the Devon and Somerset Constabulary. Other police/sportsmen include rugby

players Wade Dooley, Dean Richards and Paul Ackford who were all policemen and played together at international level 14 times for England and 2 times for the British Lions.

212.   Nick Beal and Neil Back, whose names are anagrams of each other, played rugby together for England 9 times. The partnership started successfully : the 1st time they played together was in England's 110-0 victory over the Netherlands in a qualifying match for the 1999 World Cup, which was at the time England's biggest ever margin of victory. This record was overtaken when England beat Romania 134-0 in 2001**, captained by Neil Back. Back did not score any of England's 20 tries against Romania that day, with the top scorer being Jason Robinson with 4 tries.

213.   Jason Robinson is 1 of only 4 players (along with Australians Mat Rogers and Wendell Sailor, and New Zealander Sonny Bill Williams) who have played in rugby league and rugby union World Cup Finals**. None of the 4 players has won both tournaments.

214.   Australians John Eales, Tim Horan and Jason Little, and South African Os du Randt are the only players to have won 2 Rugby Union World Cup Finals**.

215.   Os du Randt's real name is Jacobus Petrus du Randt, and he is nicknamed after the Afrikaans word os meaning ox or bullock.

216.   'The Raging Bull' was the nickname of boxer Jake LaMotta, whose autobiography was filmed as *Raging Bull*. Robert de Niro played LaMotta and won the

Academy Award for Best Actor. LaMotta appears in a cameo role in the 1961 film *The Hustler*, in which Paul Newman plays 'Fast Eddie' Felson, a pool hustler who tries to beat the legendary Minnesota Fats.

217.   The Minnesota Twins baseball team are named after the twin cities of Minneapolis and St Paul. Famous sporting twins include cricketers Sir Alec and Eric Bedser who played together for Surrey, Dutch footballers Frank and Ronald de Boer who played together at club and international level, American tennis players Bob and Mike Bryan who have won many grand slam men's doubles tournament together, Australian cricketers Mark and Steve Waugh who played together at state and international level, and US athletes Alvin and Calvin Harrison.

218.   Alvin and Calvin Harrison were both part of the 2000 Sydney Olympic Games 4 x 400m relay winning team that were subsequently disqualified after Antonio Pettigrew admitted to using performance enhancing drugs. The 4th member of the winning team was Michael Johnson who, at the same Games, became the 1st man to successfully defend the Olympic 400m title.

219.   Only 3 sportsmen have successfully defended their Olympic titles in 3 successive Games in individual sports** : Al Oerter (discus 1956 – 1968), Alexander Tikhonov (4 x 7.5km biathlon 1968 – 1980) and Carl Lewis (long jump 1984 – 1996).

220.   Despite winning 4 Olympic titles and 2 World Championships in the long jump, Carl Lewis never broke the world record.

221.   Paula Radcliffe set 2 marathon world records but won no Olympic medals.

222.   Radcliffe was the BBC Sports Personality of The Year in 2002, the year in which she set her 1st marathon world record. The 1st winner of the award was athlete Chris Chataway in 1954. Chataway had been one of the pacemakers when Sir Roger Bannister became the 1st man to break the 4 minute mile in 1954, and later became a Conservative MP from 1957-1966 and 1972-1974.

223.   Other British athletes who have been elected as politicians include double Olympic gold medallist Lord Coe (Conservative MP 1992 – 1997), and Sir Menzies Campbell, who competed in the 1964 Tokyo Olympic Games and held the British 100m record from 1967-1974 (Leader of the Liberal Democrats 2006-2007). Campbell became MP for North East Fife in 1987.

224.   In 1963 a football match in the Scottish Second Division ended in the tongue twisting Forfar Athletic 5 East Fife 4.

225.   The 1st test match of the 1979/80 Ashes included the melodic dismissal 'Lillee, caught Willey, bowled Dilley'. This was the 1st test match that the 3 had played together, and in the 4 other matches they all played in, Dilley only dismissed Lillee once more, but Paul Downton took the catch that time.

226.   Graham Dilley scored his highest test match score of 56 in the 1981 Headingley test match against Australia, in a crucial 8th wicket stand of 117 with Ian

Botham after England had followed on. This helped England gain a lead of 129 runs, and Bob Willis then took 8 for 43 as England won by 18 runs. Since test matches began in 1887, a team following on has gone on to win only 3 times**.

*Australia have been the loser in all 3 of these matches, losing to England in 1894, to England at Headingley in 1981, and to India in 2001.

227.   Cricketer/footballer Ian Botham made 11 Football League appearances for Scunthorpe United. Cricketer/footballer Phil Neale also played at Scunthorpe United, and also played with Botham at Worcestershire County Cricket Club. Phil Neale also played for Lincoln City and was playing in the match against Bradford City in May 1985 when a fire destroyed a stand and killed 56 people. Also in May 1985 his namesake Phil Neal captained Liverpool in the European Cup Final against Juventus when hooligans broke a wall that resulted in the death of 39 Juventus fans.

228.   Juventus are known as The Old Lady (La Vecchia Signora).

229.   The Bank of England is known as The Old Lady. The Bank of England Sports Centre in Roehampton, South London, hosts the Wimbledon Qualifying tournament. John McEnroe's Wimbledon debut was in 1977, when he came through the Qualifying Tournament and went on to lose to Jimmy Connors in the semi final.

230.   The 1st recorded time that John McEnroe used the phrase "You cannot be serious!" was to umpire Edward James during a 1st round Wimbledon match against Tom Gullikson in 1981. McEnroe went on to beat Bjorn Borg in the final – which brought to an end Borg's Wimbledon winning streak of 41 consecutive matches. That streak had started in 1976 against Great Britain's David Lloyd, who went on to find success in business with the David Lloyd Leisure centres.

231.   David Lloyd owns a large amount of artwork by the British micro sculptor Willard Wigan. Wigan creates sculptures that require a microscope to be seen and often fit inside the eye of a needle. One of Wigan's sculptures is 'Clay v Liston'. Cassius Clay and Sonny Liston fought twice for the World Heavyweight championship. In February 1964 Clay won by technical knockout after Liston did not start the 7th round. Shortly after the fight Clay changed his name to Muhammed Ali. In the second fight, in May 1965, Ali won with a 1st round knockout and then stood over Liston taunting him by shouting "Get up and fight, sucker!"

232.   Before the Rumble in the Jungle Ali taunted opponent George Foreman, including the memorable lines "I've tussled with a whale. I done handcuffed lightning and thrown thunder in jail. You know I'm bad. Just last week, I murdered a rock, injured a stone, hospitalized a brick."

233.   In triathlon terminology, a brick is a training workout that involves 2 of the 3 disciplines, most commonly cycling and running.

234.   An Ironman triathlon includes a 2.4m swim, a 112m mile cycle and a marathon run. The Ironman World Championship takes place every year in Hawaii. In 1997 paraplegic John McLean became the 1st wheelchair athlete to complete the Hawaii Ironman within the mandatory cut off times that able bodied athletes must achieve in order to be allowed to continue. Among his many other remarkable achievements, in 1998 McLean became the 1st wheelchair athlete to swim the English Channel.

235.   The 1st person to complete the cross Channel swim was Captain Matthew Webb in 1875. Poet Sir John Betjeman commemorated Captain Webb in his poem A Shropshire Lad. Another of Betjeman's poems, Seaside Golf, describes a golfer scoring a 3 on a hole on a links course. It is not specified in the poem whether Betjeman is playing a par 4 (and therefore scoring a birdie) or a par 5 (and therefore scoring an eagle).

236.   Birdie most probably derives from the American slang 'bird' meaning excellent. Eagle is most probably an extension of the theme used for birdie, and albatross (3 under par, called a double eagle in USA) is a further extension based on the rarity of the event and the bird. Probably the most famous albatross in golfing history was Gene Sarazen's at the 15th hole at the Masters Tournament in 1935, known as 'the shot heard round the world'. It helped him to tie for the lead and force a play off, which he went on to win. The win made him the 1st person to win each of golf's 4 major tournaments. The last major tournament that Sarazen completed was the 1973 Open Championship at Troon,

during the 1st round of which he recorded a hole in one at the 8th hole, known as the Postage Stamp.

237.   The 123 yard 8th hole at Troon was originally called Ailsa because on a clear day it gives a very good view of Ailsa Craig. Scottish golfer Willie Park Junior coined the name the Postage Stamp when writing in Golf Illustrated. Park won the Open Championship twice; his father, Willie Park Senior, won 4 Open Championships (including the inaugural Championship); and his uncle, Mungo Park, won once.

238.   Since World War Two only 2 Scottish golfers have won any major championships** : Sandy Lyle (the Open Championship and the Masters Tournament) and Paul Lawrie (the Open Championship).

239.   Lawrie won the 1999 Open Championship at Carnoustie after a play of with Justin Leonard and Jean Van de Velde. Van de Velde, needing only a double bogey at the last hole to win, took a triple bogey 7 as his ball got to the hole via the rough, the grandstand, 2 burns and a bunker in one of the most dramatic collapses in golfing history.

240.   Other famous occasions when defeat was snatched from the jaws of victory involved Greg Norman (surrendered a 6 shot lead to lose by 5 shots to Nick Faldo at the 1996 Masters), horse Devon Loch (inexplicably collapsed when 40 yards from the finish of the 1956 Grand National and with a 5 length lead), Jana Novotna (who lost the 1993 Wimbledon Ladies' Singles final after having been serving at 40-30 and 4-1 up in the final set), Don Fox (who missed a conversion in the

1968 Challenge Cup Final from in front of the posts that was the last kick of the game and would have taken the score from 10-11 to 12-11), and Steve Davis (who lost the 1985 World Snooker Championship final to Dennis Taylor 17-18 after having led 8-0).

241.   The 1st ever live televised maximum 147 break was by Steve Davis in the 1982 Lada Classic. The 1st ever live televised break at the World Championship was by Cliff Thorburn in 1983.

242.   6 players have made a maximum 147 break at the Snooker World Championship** (Cliff Thorburn, Jimmy White, Stephen Hendry, Ronnie O'Sullivan, Mark Williams and Ali Carter). In 1997 Ronnie O'Sullivan completed his maximum in a remarkable 5 minutes and 20 seconds.

243.   Ronnie O'Sullivan's nickname is The Rocket.

244.   The Rockets are Houston's NBA basketball team, who won back to back Championships in 1994 and 1995, splitting in half a run of 6 Chicago Bulls victories. In winning their 1st Championship the Rockets beat the New York Knicks. Knicks is short for Knickerbockers which is a generic term for New Yorkers.

245.   The Knickerbocker Rules, a set of rules codified by Alexander Cartwright of the New York Knickerbockers in 1845, form the basis of modern baseball's rules (although there are many significant variations to today's rules). In the 1st recorded game played under the new rules, in 1846, the

Knickerbockers were thrashed 23-1 by the New York Nine.

246.   Baseball bases are 90 feet, or 30 yards, apart.

247.   A cricket pitch (from wicket to wicket) is 22 yards long. This distance is known as a chain, based on an early piece of surveying equipment developed in the 17th century. *The Chain* was a song by Fleetwood Mac from the album *Rumours*, that was used for many years as the theme tune for the BBC's coverage of Formula One.

248.   Other famous BBC sporting theme tunes' actual titles include test match cricket (*Soul Limbo* by Booker T and the MGs), snooker (*Drag Racer* by Dog Wood Group), *Rugby Special* (*Holy Mackerel!* By Brian Bennett Band), *Ski Sunday* (*Pop Goes Bach* by New Dance Orchestra) and *Match of The Day* (*Offside* by Mike Vickers Orchestra).

249.   The 1st game shown on *Match of the Day* was Liverpool v Arsenal. Liverpool won 3-2 with the 1st goal scored by Liverpool's Roger Hunt. Hunt was a member of England's 1966 World Cup winning team and was the player who turned away to celebrate Geoff Hurst's controversial third goal rather than just knock the rebound in.

250.   Geoff Hurst is the only man to ever score a hat trick in a World Cup Final or European Championship Final**. Only 3 people have scored a hat trick in a European Cup/Champions League Final** : Alfredo di Stefano, Ferenc Puskas and Pierino Prati. Di Stefano

and Puskas scored 3 and 4 goals respectively for Real Madrid in the 7-3 thrashing of Eintracht Frankfurt in 1960. Puskas scored another hat trick in the 1963 final, when Real Madrid lost 3-5 to Benfica.

251.   Benfica were the opponents the 1st time that an English club won the European Cup, in 1968. They lost 1-4 to Manchester United, with the Manchester United goals coming from Bobby Charlton (2), Brian Kidd and George Best.

252.   George Best never played at a World Cup finals. Other great players that didn't play at a World Cup finals include George Weah, Ryan Giggs, Alfredo di Stefano, Ian Rush, Valentino Mazzola, Abedi Pele and Eric Cantona.

253.   Cantona appeared in the 1998 Academy Award nominated film *Elizabeth*. Elizabeth I's father, Henry VIII is reputed to have been playing real tennis during her mother Anne Boleyn's execution.

254.   West Ham United FC play at the Boleyn Ground (more commonly known as Upton Park), so called because Anne Boleyn is believed to have a connection with the house that originally stood on the site.

255.   West Ham United played Bolton Wanderers in the 1st ever Wembley FA Cup Final. West Ham lost 2-0 but the match is remembered as the White Horse Final after PC George Scorey and his horse Billie were instrumental in helping clear the crowd from the pitch in order to enable the match to start. Billie was actually

a grey, not a white horse, but black and white footage makes him look white.

256. Only 3 greys have ever won the Grand National**: The Lamb, Neptunes Collonges and Nicholas Silver.

257. The silver and gold medals of the 2012 Olympic Games contain the same amount of silver. The gold medal contains 1.3% gold, 92.5% silver and 6.2% copper; the silver medal contains 92.5% silver and 7.5% copper. The bronze medal contains 97% copper, 2.5% zinc and 0.5% tin.

258. *Tin Cup* is the most successful sports movie that Kevin Costner has starred in (champion power boat racer Don Johnson co-starred in the movie). Although the movie is about golf, the name comes from baseball, as explained in the movie by Tin Cup's former girlfriend Doreen : "Oh, he was the catcher on the high school baseball team. The star pitcher had a big-league curve... not all of his pitches hit Roy in the mitt, ouch. The team thought Tin Cup was a whole lot better than Clank." Kevin Costner movie *Field of Dreams* is a fantasy centred around the ghost of Shoeless Joe Jackson, who was one of the Black Sox of 1919. Other baseball movies Costner has starred in include *For the Love of the Game, Chasing Dreams* and *Bull Durham*.

259. Durham are the most recent county to have been granted first class status**, in 1991. At the start of the 2012 season, Durham's coach was Cook, the captain was Mustard, and one of the leading bowlers was Onions.

260.   Some randomly selected sports stars include German Olympic downhill skier Fanny Chmelar, German ski Jumper Andreas Wank, American baseball player Dick Pole, Olympic gold medal winning swimmer Misty Hyman, American golfer Whiffy Cox, Italian basketball player Gregor Fucka, Chinese Olympic gold medallist trampoliner Dong Dong, and American racing car driver Dick Trickle. The award, however, goes to Wolfgang Wolf who between 1998 and 2003 managed the German football club Wolfsburg.

261.   Wolfsburg grew out of a sports club for workers at Volkswagen. They have won the Bundesliga once**, in 2008/09. They qualified for the Champions League in 2009/10, when they lost 3-1 at home to Manchester United, with Michael Owen scoring a hat trick. Owen (Manchester United and Liverpool) and Fillipo Inzaghi (Juventus and Milan) are the only players to have scored hat tricks for more than 1 side in the Champions League**.

262.   There have been 41 hat tricks in test match cricket**. Hugh Trumble, Wasim Akram, Jimmy Matthews and Stuart Broad are the only players to achieve 2 hat tricks**. Matthews' was remarkable for being in the same match. He achieved the feat in each innings, and each time the final wicket was South African wicket keeper Thomas Ward. Ward died after being electrocuted in a Transvaal gold mine.

263.   Other strange and accidental sporting deaths include Payne Stewart (died in 1999 when his airplane depressurised), Vitas Gerulaitis (died of carbon monoxide poisoning in a guesthouse in 1994), Frank

Hayes (jockey who in 1923 died of a heart attack during a race at Belmont Park but still won the race), Owen Hart (professional wrestler who died after falling from almost 25m into the ring during a pre-bout stunt in 1999), all 11 players in the Democratic Republic of Congo football team Bena Tshadi (struck by lightning in 1998), and tennis linesman Dick Wertheim (who was hit by a serve from Stefan Edberg in the 1983 US Open, fell on the floor and suffered a fatal head injury). Edberg went on to win the Junior Boys' Singles title.

264.   The trophies for winners of the Men's and Women's Singles at the US Open do not have names, they are just the US Open Trophy. The other grand slam events award the Norman Brookes Challenge Cup and the Daphne Akhurst Memorial Cup (Australian Open), Coupe des Mousquetaires and Coupe Suzanne Lenglen (French Open), and the Challenge Cup and the Ladies' Singles Plate (also known as Venus Rosewater Dish) (Wimbledon).

265.   The Coupe des Mousquetaires (Musketeers' Cup) was named after 4 highly successful French tennis players known as The Four Musketeers. They were Jean Borotra, Jaques Brugnon, Henri Cochet and Rene Lacoste. Lacoste, like his contemporary Fred Perry, went on to found an extremely successful brand of sportswear. Lacoste's nickname was The Crocodile, and the Lacoste logo is a crocodile and not an alligator.

266.   The Florida Gators is the name under which various sports teams from the University of Florida compete. Famous alumni include American athlete

Frank Shorter. In 1972 Shorter won the longest Olympic running event, the marathon.

267.   'Faster, higher, stronger' is the meaning of the Olympic Movement's motto 'Citius, altius, fortius'. The Paralympic motto is 'Spirit in Motion'.

268.   *World in Motion* by Englandneworder was the official theme tune for the England team at the 1990 World Cup finals. It reached number 1 in the UK singles chart in June 1990. It was replaced at number 1 by Elton John's double A side *Sacrifice / Healing Hands*, which was his 1st number 1 after 35 other top 40 solo hits. Elton John became Chairman of Watford FC in 1976 when they were in the 4th division. He appointed future England manager Graham Taylor as manager, and the team were promoted in 1977/78, 1978/79 and to the 1st division in 1981/82. In 1981/82 and in their 1st season in the 1st division (1982/83) Luther Blissett was their top scorer.

269.   Luther Blissett is an alias used by many artists and activists since 1994. The origins are mysterious, but the practice appears to have been started by activists in Italy in 1994 (Blissett played at AC Milan in 1983 and 1984) and has spread across the world.

270.   Luther Blissett is not related to Gary Blissett, who was the Brentford footballer taken to court by Torquay United player John Uzzell after fracturing Uzzell's eye socket in an aerial challenge during a match. Blissett was acquitted of GBH.

271.   Footballers who have been convicted of assaults committed on a pitch include Duncan Ferguson (headbutted a Raith Rovers player), Eric Cantona (kung fu kicked a Crystal Palace fan after being sent off), and Joey Barton (training ground fight with Manchester City teammate Ousmane Dabo).

272.   In a 2005 Premier League match between Aston Vila and Newcastle United, Newcastle teammates Lee Bowyer and Kieron Dyer were both sent off for fighting each other when their team were losing 3-0 and already down to 10 men. Newcastle's manager that day was Graeme Souness. Souness was no stranger to controversy himself. After managing Galatasaray to victory over rivals Fenerbahce in the second leg of the Turkish Cup final, he ran on to the pitch and planted the Galatasaray flag in the Fenerbache centre circle.

273.   Turkey's Hakan Sukur scored the fastest goal in a World Cup finals match**, in the third place play off in 2002 against South Korea, timed at 11 seconds.

274.   In American football, The Turk is the name given to the man who tells aspiring players that they aren't good enough and are no longer required. Black Monday refers to both the day after the final day of the NFL season when coaching staff are fired or resign, and also to the day after the NFL draft when players contracts are terminated.

275.   Drafting order of the 32 NFL teams is determined according to their record in the previous season, with the Super Bowl losing finalists being 31st and the Super Bowl winners being 32nd.

276.   The NFL pays winning teams up to $750,000 to purchase Super Bowl rings (150 rings at up to $5,000 each)**.

277.   The parade ring is the area of a racecourse where the horse's handler will gently warm the horse up, racegoers can have a close up look at the horse before it goes onto the track, and the vet will check the horses.

278.   At Newbury racecourse in 2011, 2 horses died in the parade ring after heart attacks caused by leaking electricity from a cable that ran underneath the ring. The horses were Fenix Two and Marching Song.

279.   In 1998 Paul Gascoigne celebrated a goal for Rangers against Celtic at Celtic Park by pretending to play the flute, an instrument associated with the Loyalist Orange Order marches. Gascoigne's goal celebration cost him a £20,000 fine from his club.

280.   FIFA fined the Netherlands 15,000 Swiss Francs (about $14,500) and Spain 10,000 Swiss Francs (about $9,650) for their poor discipline in the 2010 World Cup Final. Neither team were likely to have had trouble paying the fines : Spain received $30,000,000 for winning and the Netherlands received $24,000,000 for coming second.

281.   The 2010 FIFA World Cup was played in South Africa, but South Africa didn't qualify for the knock out phase. The team's nickname is Bafana Bafana which means 'go boys, go boys'. The South African women's team is nicknamed Banyana Banyana.

282.   In a World Cup qualifying match in 2008, the South African women's cricket team beat Bermuda after only 4 legitimate deliveries of their innings. Bermuda scored 13 runs, with 10 of those coming from extras. 8 Bermudan batsmen failed to score, and the joint top scorers all scored 1 run. Opening the bowling for Bermuda, TL Paynter then sent down 9 wides and 1 no ball as South Africa won in 4 minutes after facing only 4 legitimate deliveries.

283.   The PGA Grand Slam of Golf has been held in Bermuda since 2007**. The tournament brings together the winners of the previous season's 4 majors. If a winner declines to play, or wins more than 1 tournament in a year, then the organisers invite the previous major winner with the best record in that season's majors. The event was held in America from 1979-2006, and in Bermuda from 2007. Tiger Woods won the event 5 times in a row from 1998-2002, and Ian Woosnam is the only British golfer to have won the event**, in 1991.

284.   Woosnam qualified for the Grand Slam of Golf after winning the Masters in 1991. Woosnam's Masters victory was the 4th successive win for British players after back to back wins for Nick Faldo and a win for Sandy Lyle. Inaugurated in 1934, no European had won the Masters until Seve Ballesteros in 1980, but in the 20 tournaments between 1980 and 1999, Europeans won more than half the tournaments (11 wins out of 20 tournaments), and have not won since**.

The best finish by a European since 1999 is 2nd place by Lee Westwood in 2010.

285.   Clifford Roberts was Chairman of the Augusta National Golf Course from 1931 to 1976. He once allegedly said "As long as I'm alive, all the golfers will be white and all the caddies will be black", and it was not until 1990 that Augusta invited its 1st black member. In 1975 Lee Elder became the 1st black golfer to play in the Masters. In 1977, in failing health, Roberts shot himself on Augusta's par 3 course.

286.   Albert Trott, the only batsman to ever hit the ball over the Lord's pavilion**, shot himself aged 41 after falling on hard times. Trott, like Billy Midwinter, played for both Australia (against England) and for England (against South Africa).

287.   Trott averaged 102.50 for Australia in the Ashes series of 1894/95. Several players have achieved this Ashes series milestone over the years. The most recent was England's Alastair Cook**, who averaged 127.66 in the 2010/11 Ashes. After the 4th test of the series his England teammate Jonathan Trott was also averaging over 100 (at 111.25) but a duck in England's only innings in the final test meant he ended with an average of 89.00. Whether or not Jonathan Trott is descended from Albert Trott is unsure – Jonathan Trott wrote "My grandfather always said that he was related to Albert Trott, though I never knew how".

288.   Footballers Frank Lampard and Jamie Redknapp are cousins, because their fathers Frank Lampard Senior and Harry Redknapp married twin sisters.

289.   Harry Redknapp was acquitted of tax evasion in 2012. Lester Piggott, Jesse Owens, OJ Simpson, Guus

Hiddink and Peter Graf (father of Steffi Graf) have all been convicted of tax related offences.

290.   Steffi Graf fan Gunther Parche stabbed Graf's rival Monica Seles during a match in Hamburg in 1993. The world number 1 at the time, Seles had won 8 grand slam tournaments before the stabbing, but only won 1 more. In the TV show *A Bit of Fry And Laurie*, Hugh Laurie sang a song called *I'm In Love With Steffi Graf*, including the lines "But now a shadow in the distance / A girl with a ponytail, / Sixteen and full of hunger, / The end of Steffi's trail. / I can't wait for her defeat, / I fetch a knife and take my seat. / 'Cause Steffi is a goddess, / My love for her it knows no bounds. / I'd kill to make her happy / Or just to get her through the early rounds."

291.   Steffi Graf married fellow tennis player Andre Agassi in 2001. Before Agassi, Graf dated German racing driver Michael Bartels for 7 years in the 1990s. Bartels raced in Formula One for Lotus as a stand in for Johnny Herbert in 4 Grand Prix in the 1991 season (Germany, Hungary, Italy and Spain), but failed to qualify in any. Nigel Mansell won 3 of the races in which Bartels took part, and Ayrton Senna won the other.

292.   The points system in Formula One is currently as follows : 1st (25), 2nd (18), 3rd (15), 4th (12), 5th (10), 6th (8), 7th (6), 8th (4), 9th (2), 10th (1)**. In 2014, the final race was worth double points. Between 1961 and 1990, 1st place was worth 9 points.

293. At Newcastle United the number 9 shirt is revered by fans. Wearers have included Hughie Gallacher, Len White, Wyn Davies, Malcolm Macdonald, Les Ferdinand, Micky Quinn, Alan Shearer, Andy Cole and Jackie Milburn

294. Prime Minister Tony Blair was widely ridiculed after the Sunday Sun reported him in 1997 as saying he was a Newcastle United supporter and had enjoyed watching Jackie Milburn, despite being only 4 years old and living in Australia when Milburn retired. However in 2008 the Sunday Sun confirmed that it had misquoted him, and that all he had said was that he was a Newcastle United fan and that he thought Jackie Milburn was the greatest Newcastle player of all time.

295. No Newcastle United player has ever won the European Footballer of the Year award**, although Kevin Keegan (1978 and 1979) and Michael Owen (2001) had both won the award prior to moving to Newcastle.

296. The full quote of Kevin Keegan's infamous emotional rant against Alex Ferguson during the run in of the 1995/96 season : "When you do that with footballers, like he said about Leeds, and when you do things like that about a man like Stuart Pearce, I'm... I've kept really quiet but I'll tell you something, he went down in my estimation when he said that. We have not resorted to that but I'll tell you, you can tell him now if you're watching it, we're still fighting for this title, and he's got to go to Middlesbrough and get something and, and I'll tell you honestly, I will love it if we beat them, love it." Manchester United won the title by 4

points after going to Middlesbrough on the last day of the season, winning 3-0, and getting 3 points.

297.   England beat Australia by 3 points in the 2003 rugby union World Cup Final after Jonny Wilkinson kicked a drop goal with only 28 seconds of extra time remaining. Wilkinson kicked the goal with his unfavoured right foot.

298.   In the 1st round of the 1996 World Snooker Championship, Ronnie O'Sullivan played several shots against Canadian Alain Robidoux with his unfavoured left hand, leading to Robidoux refusing to shake O'Sullivan's hand afterwards. Robidoux refused to concede the frame, despite being 57 points behind with only 22 points left on the table, and played the frame out until O'Sullivan potted the pink and won 90-41.

299.   O'Sullivan's frequently erratic behaviour was nothing compared to Australian snooker player Quentin Hann. Hann's CV includes conceding frames which he could still mathematically win, publicly challenging fellow professional Andy Hicks to a fight after a match, aimlessly smashing the pack of reds during matches, having to play without shoes after breaking his foot in a parachute jump, playing with a hangover in the World Championships ("By the end I was in bits"), being tried twice for sex offences, and being banned for 8 years after being found guilty of agreeing to throw a match against Ken Doherty.

300.   Peter O'Sullevan, the BBC's leading horseracing commentator for much of the second half of the 20th century, spelt his surname with an E and not an I.

O'Sullevan commentated on the coverage of many Grand Nationals, including Red Rum's 3 victories, the void race of 1993, and the 1956 race when Devon Loch stumbled when only yards from the finish. Devon Loch's jockey in the race was Dick Francis, who went on to become a bestselling crime novelist. Francis' 1st book was an autobiography entitled The Sport of Queens.

301.   Queens in New York City is the location of the New York Mets baseball team. The Mets have won 2 World Series, compared to 27 wins by cross town rivals the New York Yankees**.

302.   The World Series is the end of season best of 7 match series played between the winners of the American League and the National League. Played in October, it is also known as the Fall Classic.

303.   At the 1984 Los Angeles Olympic Games, World Champion and home favourite Mary Decker fell during the 3000m final after a collision with Britain's barefooted Zola Budd. Budd was South African and been fast tracked to British citizenship in 1984 (her grandfather was British) in order to be able to compete in the Games, at a time when South Africa was banned from competing in international sport.

304.   In 1982, the squad of England cricketers that took part on a rebel tour to South Africa was : Graham Gooch (captain), Dennis Amiss, Geoffrey Boycott, John Emburey, Mike Hendrick, Geoff Humpage, Alan Knott, Wayne Larkins, John Lever, Chris Old, Arnold Sidebottom, Les Taylor, Derek Underwood, Peter Willey and Bob Woolmer.

305.	Woolmer went on to become the coach of the Pakistan national team. During the 2007 World Cup he was found dead in his room at the Pegasus Hotel in Kingston, Jamaica. Despite many rumours of foul play, and a murder investigation, an open verdict was recorded on his death.

306.	In the 1985 Bond film *A View To A Kill*, in scenes filmed at Ascot racecourse in Berkshire, a microchip planted in the horse Pegasus enables it to accelerate away from the field and win the race.

307.	Australian George Lazenby, who played Bond in the 1969 film *On Her Majesty's Secret Service*, is divorced from former US tennis player Pam Shriver. Shriver won 21 grand slam doubles titles with Martina Navratilova.

308.	Between 1982 and 1996, Steffi Graf and/or Martina Navratilova appeared in 83% of grand slam singles finals.

309.	Between 2004 and 2011, Roger Federer and/or Rafael Nadal appeared in 87.5% of grand slam singles finals.

310.	Miguel Angel Nadal, Rafael Nadal's uncle, missed the decisive last penalty in the quarter final shootout against England at Euro '96. Only Stuart Pearce and Frank Lampard know what it feels like to score and also to miss a penalty for England in a penalty shoot out. Michael Owen, Alan Shearer, David Platt and Owen Hargreaves have both taken 2 and scored 2.

311.	Owen Hargreaves is Canadian by birth. Other famous Canadian sportsmen who took British citizenship include Greg Rusedski and Lennox Lewis.

312.	Lennox Lewis's middle name is Claudius, who was the 4th Roman Emperor. Nero succeeded Claudius as Emperor. Former England rugby captain Lawrence Dallaglio's middle names are Bruno Nero.

313.	In 1993 Frank Bruno lost to Lennox Lewis in a fight for Lewis' WBC heavyweight title. In 1995 Bruno won the title after beating champion Oliver McCall. Lewis fought McCall twice : in 1994 he lost his WBC heavyweight title to McCall, but in 1997, when McCall challenged Lewis for the title that Lewis then held, the fight was stopped after McCall repeatedly refused to defend himself and started crying.

314.	In the 1989 FA Cup Final Everton's Stuart McCall became the 1st substitute to score twice in an FA Cup Final. However within 2 minutes Ian Rush became the second player to achieve the feat. Ian Wright became the third player to achieve it in the following year's final and these 3 remain the only players to have achieved the feat**.

315.	The 1st FA Cup final was played at the Oval in 1872. Other than The Oval, the only ground to have hosted an FA Cup Final and a cricket test match is Bramall Lane in Sheffield. It hosted the 1902 test match between England and Australia and the 1912 FA Cup Final replay between Barnsley and West Bromwich Albion.

316.   West Bromwich Albion's ground, The Hawthorns, is at a higher altitude than any other English professional football team's ground**. It is 168 metres above sea level.

317.   3 of the 4 main characters in BBC TV show *New Tricks* - Jack Halford, Brian Lane and Gerry Standing - are named after WBA's Halford's Lane Stand (now known as the West Stand). In the show, Brian Lane is an avid AFC Wimbledon fan, as is the actor that plays him, Alun Armstrong.

318.   Footballer Alun Armstrong scored the winning goal for Ipswich Town FC against Inter Milan in the 2001/02 UEFA Cup. In European competition, Ipswich have played Italian opposition 4 times**, winning every home game and losing every away game against Inter Milan, AC Milan, Lazio and Roma.

319.   Ipswich's European competition opponents all ground share** : AC Milan and Inter both play at the San Siro, and Roma and Lazio both play at the Stadio Olimpico, which hosted the opening and closing ceremonies and the athletics events during the 1960 Rome Olympic Games.

320.   Abebe Bikila from Ethiopia won the 1960 Olympic marathon running barefoot. He defended his title at the 1964 Olympics, when he decided to run in shoes. Bikila's 1960 victory was Ethiopia's 1st Olympic medal, and since then they have won 44 more medals, each being in long distance running events (the marathon, 10,000m, 5,000m and the 3,000m steeplechase)**.

321.	During a 3,000m steeplechase the winner has to jump 28 barriers and 7 water jumps. The Grand National steeplechase is 7,200m and has 25 barriers and 5 water jumps (16 fences including Becher's Brook and Valentine's Brook, all jumped twice except The Water Jump and The Chair).

322.	When Paul Gascoigne scored for England against Scotland in Euro '96, he celebrated by re-enacting the dentist's chair drinking game which had caused much furore during the pre-tournament tour of the Far East. Alan Shearer was the player to squirt the water bottle into Gazza's mouth as Jamie Redknapp and Steve McManaman looked on.

323.	Other famously ill-advised goal celebrations include Liverpool's Robbie Fowler pretending to snort cocaine from the byline after equalising from the penalty spot against Everton in 1999 (£60,000 fine) and Diego Maradona's mad bulging eyes dash towards the pitchside camera after scoring for Argentina against Greece at the 1994 FIFA World Cup finals. Maradona played 1 more game for Argentina, but was subsequently banned after a positive test for ephedrine and never played again for Argentina.

324.	In 1996 Fowler tried to persuade a referee to reverse a penalty that had been given in his favour, claiming that Arsenal goalkeeper David Seaman had not fouled him. The penalty stood, Fowler's effort was saved, but Jason McAteer scored the rebound.

325.	McAteer and Fowler were 2 of the so called Spice Boys, along with Steve McManaman, Jamie

Redknapp and David James. The term was intended to convey their status as underachieving playboys. David Beckham, who married Spice Girl Victoria Adams, was never one of the Spice Boys.

326.   Victoria Beckham's dad is called Tony Adams.

327.   Footballer Tony Adams spent his entire senior playing career at Arsenal. Other players who completed their entire senior career at 1 club include Giuseppe Bergomi (Inter Milan), Matt Le Tissier (Southampton), Nat Lofthouse (Bolton Wanderers), Billy McNeill (Celtic), Jack Charlton (Leeds United), Franco Baresi (AC Milan) and Paolo Maldini (AC Milan).

328.   Maldini is one of only 2 players (along with Francisco Gento) who has appeared in 8 European Cup/Champions League finals**, and he has won 5. In 2003 and 2007 Maldini played with Clarence Seedorf, who is the only player to have won the tournament with 3 different clubs** (Real Madrid, AC Milan and Ajax).

329.   In 2007 Ajax took the unusual step of retiring shirt number 14 in honour of Johan Cruyff who scored 190 goals in 240 performances for them between 1964 and 1973.

330.   Cruyff perfected the 'Cruyff turn', whereby he would look to pass or cross then drag the ball behind his standing foot and move off at 180 degrees. The most replayed example occurred against Sweden in the 1974 FIFA World Cup finals. The blue-shorted defender

who was left perplexed was Jan Olsson. Cruyff's turn didn't result in a goal and the game ended 0-0.

331.   The last rugby union international match to end 0-0 was Togo versus Nigeria in 2004**. The last match to end 0-0 involving a home nation was Scotland versus New Zealand in 1964**. Scotland have never beaten New Zealand**. They have played 30 times, lost 28 times and drawn twice*. The other draw was in 1983 when the match finished 25-25.

332.   The 1st Twenty20 cricket international was between New Zealand and Australia in 2005. The match was semi-serious, with players turning out in retro kit, some sporting retro facial hair and Glenn McGrath replaying the famous Trevor Chappell underarm bowling incident from 1981. Australia won the match, meaning that they had won the inaugural test (1877), the inaugural one day international (1971) and the inaugural Twenty20 match. The man of the match was Ricky Ponting.

333.   In the 2005 Ashes test match at Trent Bridge, substitute fielder Gary Pratt ran out Ponting, leading to a tirade from Ponting against the England coach Duncan Fletcher and the rest of the playing staff on the England balcony as he left the field. Ponting's outburst was misplaced as, although England has been bending the rules with their use of substitute fielders throughout the series, Pratt was legitimately on for Simon Jones who was on his way to hospital with an ankle injury which ended his international career.

334.   Jones played for England, even though he is Welsh, because the ECB is actually the England and Wales Cricket Board and England and Wales join together to play cricket. 2 Welshmen have captained the England cricket team – Tony Lewis (9 tests, 8 as captain) and Cyril Walters (11 tests, 1 as captain)**.

335.   The Ireland cricket and rugby teams represent both the Republic of Ireland and Northern Ireland. Cricketer Eoin Morgan has played for Ireland against England (in the 2007 World Cup), and has also played for England against Ireland (as captain in a match in 2011). Irishman Ed Joyce qualified to play for England through residency and played 17 times for England in 2006/07, including 2 matches against Ireland. In his debut, against Ireland, he played against his brother who was Ireland's opening batsman. Since failing to be picked for England, Joyce was given special dispensation by the ICC to play for Ireland. He has played 2 matches against England since, including Ireland's 1st ever victory over England in the 2011 World Cup. Therefore in the 2007 World Cup Joyce played for England against Morgan playing for Ireland, and in 2011 Joyce played for Ireland against Morgan playing for England.

336.   The cricket World Cup has been won by Australia (4 times), West Indies (twice), India (twice), Pakistan (once), and Sri Lanka (once)*. England are the only team who have reached a final (3 times) but never won a final**. The 1996 final, won by Sri Lanka, was held in the Gadaffi Stadium, name after assassinated Libyan leader Colonel Muammar al-Gadaffi.

337.   In 2009 the Sri Lankan cricket team was travelling to the Gadaffi Stadium when it was ambushed by gunmen who killed 6 policemen and 2 civilians. Among those on the bus were English match referee Chris Broad. Broad's most remembered act on a cricket field is when he knocked over the leg stump of his wicket by hitting it with his bat after being bowled by Steve Waugh in the 1998 Bicentennial test match at Sydney – he had just scored 139.

338.   Waugh and Marvan Atapattu share the record for the most ducks in test cricket by a recognised batsman, with 22 each**. Waugh's nickname was Tugga Waugh.

339.   Tug o' War was an Olympic sport and was last contested at the Antwerp Games in 1920. Other discontinued Olympic sports, and their last Olympic appearance, include 100m freestyle swim for Greek sailors (1896), swimming obstacle race (1900), live pigeon shooting (1900), equestrian high jump and long jump (1900), and the 2 handed javelin and 2 handed discus (3 throws with the right hand, 3 throws with the left hand, best distance with each hand gives aggregate total) (1912).

340.   Right handed boxers are called orthodox and left handed boxers are called southpaw. The term southpaw comes from baseball. Early ballparks had the home plate facing east so that the afternoon sun would not blind the batter. If the pitcher was left handed, the ball would be thrown with his south side hand, i.e. with his south paw.

341.   All of the British Classics (except the 1,000 and 2,000 Guineas) and the major National Hunt races (the Grand National at Aintree and the Cheltenham Gold Cup at Cheltenham) are run on left handed racecourses. Newmarket, that hosts the 1,000 and 2,000 Guineas is right handed and has 2 courses : the Rowley Mile Course and the July Course.

342.   The St Leger is the oldest of The Classics, having first run in 1776. It has taken place every year except 1939. It is also the longest of the Classics, at 1m 6 furlongs and 132 yards. The shortest Classics are the 1,000 and 2,000 Guineas, both raced over 1 mile.

343.   A furlong is 1/8th of a mile, or 200m.

344.   Paul Furlong was a footballer who made 59 appearances for Chelsea in 1994-1996. His last game in May 1996 was also manager Glenn Hoddle's last game and marked a watershed for Chelsea : ignoring caretaker managers, Chelsea had only ever had British managers until that match, and have only ever had foreign managers since.

345.   Under Gullit's Italian successor, Gianluca Vialli, Chelsea became the 1st British team to field a starting 11 with no British or Irish players, against Southampton in December 1999. The starting line up was De Goey (Holland), Petrescu (Romania), Thome (Brazil), Leboeuf (France), Babayaro (Nigeria), Ferrer (Spain), Deschamps (France), Poyet (Uruguay), Di Matteo (Italy), Ambrosetti (Italy), and Flo (Norway).

346.   Deschamps and Leboeuf, along with other Chelsea/France players Emmanuel Petit and Marcel Desailly, has been part of the French team that won the 1998 World Cup Final. For that tournament, future Chelsea player Nicolas Anelka had not been selected. Anelka was not selected for the 1998, 2002 or 2006 World Cup finals. When he was finally selected for the 2010 tournament, he played in the 1st match, was substituted at half time during the second match (a 2-0 defeat to Mexico) and subsequently sent home after insulting the manager. Despite his lack of World Cup success, Anelka has won the European Championship, the Champions League, the Premier League and FA Cup. Anelka is one of only 6 players to have won the Premier League with more than 1 club (Chelsea and Arsenal), along with Gael Clichy (Arsenal and Manchester City), Ashley Cole (Arsenal and Chelsea), Henning Berg (Blackburn Rovers and Manchester United), Carlos Tevez (Manchester United and Manchester City) and Kolo Toure (Arsenal and Manchester City)**.

347.   Only 1 player has won the FIFA World Cup, European Championship, the Champions League, the Premier League and the FA Cup** : Thierry Henry. Patrick Vieira won the FIFA World Cup, European Championship, the Premier League and the FA Cup, and played twice as a substitute for Internazionale in the 2009/10 Champions League which they went on to win, but did not receive a winner's medal.

**Of current players, 4 are missing one of the set :
Gerard Pique (FA Cup), Fernando Torres (Premier*

League), Juan Mata (Premier League) and David Silva (Champions League).

348.	Thierry Henry played in America's Major League Soccer at the end of his career, with the New York Red Bulls. Other players who have cashed in by playing in America at the end of their careers include Pele, Franz Beckenbauer, Johann Cruyff, Alan Ball, George Best, Trevor Francis, Archie Gemmill, Johnny Giles, Bruce Grobbelaar, Geoff Hurst, Rodney Marsh, Gerd Muller, Johan Neeskens, Peter Osgood, Rivelino, Frans Thijssen, Ricky Villa, Frank Worthington and Terry Yorath. Unusually, Peter Beardsley played for the Vancouver Whitecaps at the start of his career before transferring to Newcastle United.

349.	Peter Beardsley moved directly from Liverpool to rivals Everton in 1991. Other players to have moved directly from one club to the other include Abel Xavier, Gary Ablett, Kevin Sheedy and Nick Barmby.

350.	Nick Barmby scored the 1st competitive goal of the eras of both England managers Glenn Hoddle and Sven Goran Eriksson.

351.	Nick Barmby was born in Hull, played 180 times for Hull City and has been their manager. Hull City is the only British Football League team none of whose letters can be coloured in. Hull City's celebrity fan club consists of actor Omar Shariff (also a world class bridge player) and English actor Tom Courtenay.

352.	Courtenay starred in the 1962 film *The Loneliness of The Long Distance Runner*, about a young man in borstal who gains prestige through his prowess at cross country running. In the key race against a local public school, Courtenay is winning easily but in an act of rebellion against the borstal and the governor, stops a few yards short of the finish line and waits, allowing the public school's runner to win.

353. In the 1908 London Olympic Games marathon, Dorando Pietri of Italy entered the stadium first but collapsed several times and ran the wrong way. 2 officials helped Pietri up when he fell, and despite finishing 1st Pietri was disqualified because of the help he had received. Pietri was later awarded a special cup by Queen Alexandra in recognition of his achievement and the fact that he had not been responsible for his disqualification.

354. At the 1992 Barcelona Olympics, after posting the quickest time in the 1st round and winning his quarter final, Britain's Derek Redmond tore a hamstring during the semi final of the men's 400m. Hobbling the second half of the race, Redmond's father ran on to the track and helped him for the last 100m, and a tearful Redmond received a standing ovation at the finish. Like Pietri, Redmond was officially disqualified as he had been helped to the finish. After athletics, Redmond played basketball for England.

355. In arguably the most controversial ending to an Olympic match in any team sport, the Soviet Union beat the USA in the 1972 Olympic basketball final 51-50, with Sergei Belov scoring the winning basket with the final play of the match. The final few seconds of the match were mired in controversy and confusion around

the time remaining and time outs. As a result of the controversy the USA refused to accept their silver medals and have never relented. It was the 1ˢᵗ time that USA had lost an Olympic basketball match in their 63 games since the sport was inaugurated at the 1936 Olympics. Since then they have played 71 games and lost 4 times}, to the Soviet Union (1988), and in 2004 to Puerto Rico, Argentina and Lithuania, where basketball is the most popular sport.

356.   Lithuania held the record for the most consecutive international rugby union victories, with 17, until Cyprus overtook their record.

357.   Australia hold the record for the most consecutive test match victories** (16) and Spain hold the record for the most consecutive international football victories** (15).

358.   Spain's streak lasted from 26ᵗʰ June 2008 until 24ᵗʰ June 2009, and started with the semi final win over Russia at the 2008 European Championships. 3 Barcelona players played in that match – Carlos Puyol, Andres Iniesta and Xavi - and over the next 3 years these players won the 2008 European Championship, the 2008/09 Spanish League and 2008/09 Champions League, the 2009/10 Spanish League and 2010 World Cup, the 2010/11 Spanish League and 2010/11 Champions League. The only blot on their record was Barcelona's failure to win the 2009/10 Champions League, when they lost in the semi final to Inter Milan.

359.   *Barcelona* was the song recorded by Queen's Freddie Mercury and Spanish opera singer Monserrat

Caballe, written for the 1992 Barcelona Olympic Games. Originally released in 1987, it was rereleased in 1992 for the Olympics (after Mercury's death in 1991), reaching number 2 both times in the UK chart.

360.   Queen Elizabeth II, Adolf Hitler and Emperor Hirohito are the only people to have opened more than 1 Olympic Games**. The Queen opened the 1976 Montreal games and 2012 London games (but Prince Philip opened the 1956 Melbourne Olympics, Governor General Sir William Deane opened the 2000 Sydney Olympics and Governor General Michaelle Jean opened the 2010 Vancouver Olympics).

361.   The Montreal Olympics were the most recent Summer Olympic games at which the host country (Canada) failed to win a gold medal**.

362.   The Calgary Olympics in 1988 were the most recent Winter Olympic games at which the host country (Canada, again) failed to win a gold medal**.

363.   Lacrosse is the oldest sport still played today in North America, and has its origins in games played by native Indians in modern day Canada. The game was played as a sport as well as a means of training warriors, with games sometimes lasting up to 3 days, with goals occasionally several miles apart. The game is so called after Jesuit missionary Jean de Brebeuf in 1636 saw the game and likened the stick being used to a bishop's crozier (la crosse in French).

364.   Adam Crozier was Chief Executive of the Football Association when they appointed England's 1st foreign

manager, Sven Goran Eriksson. After leaving England Eriksson had spells managing Manchester City and Leicester City, with brief spells at Mexico (9 games) and Ivory Coast (23 games) sandwiched in between. Other globetrotting international managers include.

Bora Milutinovic** 8 : Mexico, Costa Rica, USA, Nigeria, China, Honduras, Jamaica and Iraq

Philippe Troussier** 7 : Cote d'Ivoire, Nigeria, South Africa, Burkina Faso, Japan, Qatar and Morocco

Carlos Alberto Parreira** 6 : Brazil, Ghana, Kuwait, United Arab Emirates, Saudi Arabia and South Africa

Guus Hiddink 5** : Holland, South Korea, Australia, Russia and Turkey

Bruno Metsu** 4 : Guinea, Senegal, United Arab Emirates and Qatar

365.   Luiz Felipe Scolari managed Brazil when they knocked England out of the 2002 World Cup, and managed Portugal when they knocked England out of Euro 2004 and the 2006 World Cup, and so took care of England for 3 successive tournaments.

366.   In every rugby union World Cup between 1991 and 2007, Australia either won (1991, 1999) or were knocked out by England (1995, 2003, 2007).

367.   The rugby league World Cup started in 1954. The trophy was stolen, shortly before the final of the 1970 tournament, from the Midland Hotel in Bradford,

Yorkshire. The trophy was not found again until 1990 in a Bradford rubbish tip, its whereabouts for 20 years remaining a mystery. The trophy was being replaced by a new one in 1970 anyway, but after its rediscovery was used again as the main trophy for the 2000 and 2008 tournaments.

368.   At the George Hotel in Huddersfield, Yorkshire in 1895, 21 clubs formed the Northern Rugby Football Union. Rule changes that created differences between rugby union and rugby league were introduced in stages over many years (e.g. 13 players, no line out, playing the ball instead of a scrum).

369.   Australia have finished either 1st or 2nd in every rugby league World Cup except the 1st one in 1954**.

370.   The top scorer in the 1954 tournament was Gordon Brown, who was not the Scottish Rugby Union international who played for the Lions on the 1974 tour of South Africa nor the British Prime Minister of the same name.

371.   The Stanley Cup was donated by the governor general of Canada, Lord Stanley of Preston in 1892 as the Dominion Hockey Challenge Cup. Stanley was the son of Prime Minister Edward Smith-Stanley, and was himself a Conservative MP between 1865-1886. From 1885-1886 the future Lord Stanley was MP for Blackpool.

372.   Sir Stanley Matthews, who played most of his career at Blackpool, is the only footballer to have been knighted while still playing**. Matthews played his last

professional game less than a week after his 50th birthday.

373.   Teddy Sheringham is the oldest player to have scored in the Premier League** (when 40 years old for West Ham United v Portsmouth in 2006). Sheringham scored the 1st ever live goal on Sky Sports, for Nottingham Forest against Liverpool in August 1992.

374.   One of Nottingham Forest's unofficial nicknames is the Tricky Trees.

375.   2 cricket grounds used regularly for first class cricket have a tree within the playing area. At Kent County Cricket Club's St Lawrence ground in Canterbury, the original lime tree was felled by wind in 2005, but was replaced soon after. The City Oval in Pietermaritzburg, South Africa, also has a tree within the field of play. Balls hitting the trees always count as 4, and a batsman cannot be caught off the tree.

376.   Law 32 of cricket states that if an umpire believes a batsman to be dismissed in more than 1 way in the same delivery, 'caught out' takes precedence over all other methods of dismissal except bowled.

377.   A googly is a delivery by a right handed leg spin bowler that spins from off stump towards leg stump.

378.   A chinaman is a delivery by a left handed spin bowler that spins from off stump towards leg stump. The term comes from a match in 1933 between England and West Indies, when Walter Robins was stumped off such a delivery from Elliss Achong, the 1st

test match player of Chinese origin. Robins is reported to have commented to the umpire as he left "Fancy being done by a bloody Chinaman!".

379.   Yao Ming, who carried the Chinese flag during the opening ceremony of the 2004 Athens Olympic Games, is the 4th tallest NBA player of all time at 7 ft 6 in**. One of the 2 tallest players of all time**, 7 ft 7 in Manute Bol, played alongside the shortest player of all time**, 5 ft 3 in Muggsy Bogues, for the Washington Bullets.

380.   Since 1928 at the Opening Ceremony of the Olympic Games, the delegations parade in alphabetical order according to the language of the host country, except for Greece, which always leads the parade, and for the host country, which always brings up the rear. As Greece were hosting the Olympics in 2004, their flag bearer entered first and the rest of the delegation paraded last.

381.   Before the 1st FIFA World Cup in 1930, Uruguay had won the football gold medal at the 1928 and 1924 Games. Football tournaments had been held in the Olympics since 1900 but only with a mixture of club or scratch teams, and then only European national teams. 1924 saw the 1st truly international tournament at the Games.

382.   Harald Bohr, Danish mathematician and brother of Nobel prize winning physicist Niels Bohr, won a silver medal with the Danish football team at the 1908 Olympics in London. Bohr scored twice in the quarter final 9-0 demolition of France B, but failed to find the

net in the 17-1 semi final win over France A in which teammate Sophus Nielsen scored 10 times (an Olympic record), including a hat trick within the game's opening 6 minutes.

383.   The most goals scored in a World Cup Finals match is 5** by Oleg Salenko for Russia against Cameroon in 1994. The most in a qualifying match is 13** by Australia's Archie Thompson in the 31-0 qualifying group victory against American Samoa in 2002. In their qualifying campaign, Australia's other matches ended 22-0 (v Tonga), 11-0 (v Samoa) and 2-0 (v Fiji). The Socceroos fell at the final qualifying hurdle, losing a 2 legged play off Uruguay having already won a 2 legged play off against New Zealand, so were eliminated despite a goal difference of +69.

384.   In the 2010 World Cup, pre-tournament 2,000 to 1 rank outsiders New Zealand ended up as the only undefeated team. They were eliminated after drawing all 3 games, (and eventual winners Spain lost their opening game to Switzerland). The only other tournament this has happened in was in 1974** where Scotland were eliminated without losing and eventual winners West Germany lost a group game to East Germany.

385.   1974 was the only World Cup in which East Germany played. Other teams that have only appeared in 1 World Cup Finals are Angola, Bosnia and Herzegovina, Canada, China, Democratic Republic of Congo (as Zaire), Cuba, Haiti, Indonesia (as Dutch East Indies), Iraq, Israel, Jamaica, Kuwait, Senegal, Togo, Trinidad & Tobago, UAE, Ukraine and Wales*.

386.   In 2022 Qatar will appear in the Finals for the 1st time by virtue of being hosts (assuming they fail to qualify for 2018 tournament). The average daily maximum temperature in Qatar in June and July in 41 degrees centigrade, sometimes reaching 50 degrees, Qatar has a population (1.6m) almost exactly half the number of spectators that watched the 2010 World Cup Finals (3.2m). Israel may struggle to add to their one appearance to date, as Qatar does not officially recognize the country.

387.   Qatar has led the way in buying foreign athletes, mainly from Kenya, in order to achieve success in athletics. High profile purchases include World Championship gold medallist Stephen Cherono, Albert Chepkurui,   David Nyaga, Onèsphore Nkunzimana, Moses Kipkirui, Daniel Kipkosgei, Thomas Katui, Richard Yatich and Elijah Kosgei. Or as they are now cunningly known : Saif Saaeed Shaheen, Ahmad Hassan Abdullah, Daham Najim Bashir, Sultan Khamis Zaman, Musa Amer Obaid, Essa Ismail Rashed, Gamal Belal Salem, Mubarak Hassan Shami and Majed Saeed Sultan.

388.   'The Sultan of Swat' was one of George Herman Ruth's nicknames, along with 'Babe Ruth' and 'The Bambino'. Ruth's 1st club was the then minor league Baltimore Orioles. An oriole is a type of bird.

389.   Other team nicknames whose meanings are not immediately obvious include NFL team Cleveland Browns (named after 1st coach, Paul Brown), the Owls (Sheffield Wednesday FC, named after the ground's location in Owlerton), the Addicks (Charlton Athletic FC, a corruption of haddocks, in honour of a local fish and

chip shop), and the Bhoys (Celtic FC, a corruption of The Boys, to make it sound more Irish). The unofficial nickname of Hartlepool United FC – the Monkey Hangers – derives from a story dating from the time of the Napoleonic Wars when a monkey was found as the only survivor of a French shipwreck. The story has it that the monkey as found dressed in a French uniform, presumably in order to amuse the crew, and was promptly tried and hanged as a spy. The club's mascot, H'Angus The Monkey, was successfully elected as the Mayor of Hartlepool in 2002 (running under his own name) and was re-elected after stopping wearing his mascot uniform and starting taking politics seriously.

390.   Other British people who have been involved in both sport and politics over their careers include : double Olympic gold medallist athlete, Chairman of the organizing committee of the London 2012 Olympic Games, and Conservative MP and peer Sebastian Coe; Olympic silver medallist rower, British Olympic Association Chairman, and Conservative MP and peer Colin Moynihan; TV sports presenter, former Green Party spokesman, and new age conspiracy theorist David Icke; British number 1 tennis player, National Front supporter, unsuccessful parliamentary candidate for the Conservative Party and UKIP support Buster Mottram; international fencer, Conservative and Labour MP, and Leader of the British Union of Fascists Oswald Mosley; world champion boxer and independent parliamentary candidate (under the legal name of 'None of the Above X') Terry Marsh. On his website Jeffrey Archer (Conservative MP and peer, and Deputy Chairman of the party) claims to have

represented Great Britain and run 100 yards in 9.6 seconds in 1966.

391.   The posh name for archery is toxophily (from the ancient Greek meaning 'love of arrows'). Someone that makes or sells arrows is a fletcher.

392.   Duncan Fletcher was England coach when England won the Ashes for the 1st time in 18 years in 2005. This ended the second longest period of time for which 1 team had continuously held the Ashes. The longest period of Ashes dominance was from 1934 until 1953** (3 days short of 19 years), although no matches were played between 1938 and 1946. When England regained the Ashes with a 1-0 series win in 1953, Denis Compton hit the winning runs.

393.   The Compton-Miller medal, named after Compton and Australian Keith Miller, is awarded to the player of the series in each Ashes series. Since its inauguration in 2005, the winners have been Andrew Flintoff, Ricky Ponting, Andrew Strauss, Alistair Cook, Ian Bell and Mitchell Johnson*.

394.   In the 1st test match at Brisbane in 2009, Cook spent all but 11.2 overs of the 5 day match on the field. The ground in Brisbane, called The Gabba, is an abbreviation of Woolloongabba, the area of the city in which the ground is situated. The ground is often referred to as The Gabbatoir, such is England's dismal record there : England have won 2 tests there since 1946, out of 18 played*.

395.   Only 2 test matches, out of over 2,000 played, have ended in a tie** : the matches between Australia and West Indies at The Gabba in 1960, and between India and Australia in Chennai in 1986.

396.   7 test matches have been officially abandoned, all due to prolonged fog or rain that forced the matched to be abandoned without a ball being bowled**. Other test matches that have finished in unusual circumstances include:

England v Pakistan at the Oval in 2006 : Pakistan refused to continue playing shortly after umpire Darrell Hair penalised Pakistan 5 runs for ball tampering. England were later awarded the match victory.

Pakistan v England at Karachi in 1969 : Match abandoned as a draw after 2 days, following rioting.

West Indies v England at Jamaica 1998 : Match abandoned as a draw after 10.1 overs after pitch was declared too unpredictable and dangerous to play.

England v Australia at Headingley in 1975 : Match abandoned as a draw after the pitch was vandalised before the last day by supporters of convicted bank robber George Davis.

397.   George Davis is referred to on the song *Friends of Mine* on Duran Duran's eponymous 1981 debut album. Duran Duran's lead singer, Simon Le Bon, took part in the 1985 Fastnet yachting race (where he and the crew had to be rescued after capsizing). He also competed in the 1985-86 Whitbread Round the World

Race (finishing third) and in the 2005 Fastnet race (did not finish).

398.   During the 1979 Fastnet race, violent storms led to the deaths of 15 competitors, the worst yachting race disaster of all time. The Fastnet race starts at Cowes and ends at Plymouth Hoe.

399.   Sir Francis Drake was on Plymouth Hoe playing bowls when first told of the impending arrival of the Spanish Armada. Folklore says he responded that there was plenty of time to finish the game and beat the Spanish.

400.   The ball in bowls is called a bowl, or also a wood.

401.   On his way to victory at the 2006 Open Championship, Tiger Woods only used his 1 wood (driver) off the tee once. His strategy of sacrificing distance for greater accuracy in hitting fairways and avoiding bunkers was rewarded with victory.

402.   There are 967 bunkers on The Straits Course at Whistling Straits in Wisconsin**. The amount of sand caused controversy at the 2012 USPGA Championship. At the 18th hole, leader Dustin Johnson hit his drive into what he thought was rough, and ended with a bogey to tie for the lead. As he left the green it was pointed out to him that his ball had been in a bunker and he had grounded his club, thereby incurring a 2 stroke penalty. As a result, he dropped out of the play off and tied 5th. 5th place got him $271k, whereas winning the play off would have won him $1.35m.

403.   The winner of the USPGA the only other time it has been held at Whistling Straits**, in 2004, was Vijay Singh. For years Singh has been dogged by allegations of cheating relating to the 1985 Indonesian Open where the Tournament Director decided Singh had improved his score (given to him by his playing partner) by 1 stroke before signing his scorecard. Singh was disqualified from the tournament and suspended indefinitely by the Southeast Asia Golf Federation.

404.   Singh has won 2 majors other than the 2004 USPGA at Whistling Straits** : the USPGA Championship in 1998 and the 2000 Masters. Since the inaugural Masters in 1934 (and excluding 1939-1945), the 2000 season when Singh won is 1 of only 4 years in which none of golf's majors have been won by a player winning their 1st major** : 1972, 1980, 2000 and 2014. In 2000 Tiger Woods won the other 3 majors, and he also won the 2001 Masters, and so completed the 'Tiger Slam' by holding all 4 of golf's major trophies at the same time but not from 1 season. No player has ever won all 4 trophies in the same season**.

405.   Colin Montgomerie is generally considered to be the best golfer never to have won a major. He came second or tied second 5 times in majors, including 2 play off defeats. In the Ryder Cup Montgomerie did not lose a singles match in 8 appearances, and captained Europe to victory in 2010. The 2010 Ryder Cup team contained brothers Francesco and Edoardo Molinari, the 4th time that brothers had played on the same Ryder Cup team (after 2 Whitcombe brothers in 1929 and 1931, 3 Whitcombe brothers in 1935, and 2 Hunt brothers in 1963).

406.   In the 2010 and 2014 FIFA World Cups half-brothers Jerome Boateng and Kevin-Prince Boateng played against each other when Germany played Ghana. Germany won 1-0 in 2010 and it finished 2-2 in 2014.

407.   Germany have the best record in World Cup Finals penalty shoot outs** (4 out of 4) and England have the worst record** (0 out of 3). England's individual penalty success rate is 50% in World Cup shoot outs, with 14 kicks taken and 7 missed*.

408.   West Germany have had 1 World Cup shoot out against England, in the semi final in 1990**. In that tournament they went on to win the final 1-0 against Argentina with a penalty, meaning that they had won the tournament without ever being behind at any stage in any game in the tournament. The only other winners to have achieved this feat are Italy (in both 1938 and 1982)**.

409.   Socrates captained Brazil against Italy (and scored) in 1982. Socrates only ever played for 2 clubs outside of Brazil – Fiorentina in Italy and West Yorkshire team Garforth Town AFC, coming on as substitute and playing for a few minutes against Tadcaster Albion in November 2004.

410.   New Zealand flanker Jerry Collins was on holiday after the 2007 Rugby World Cup, when Barnstaple rugby club's coach spotted him and invited him to come and watch a game. To everyone's surprise Collins turned up, so they then asked him to run a coaching session. The following weekend Collins played for the

club's 2nd XV in a match against Newton Abbott (having bought some boots from a sports shop), and then wore Barnstaple socks when he played for the Barbarians against South Africa a few weeks later.

411.   The Barbarian Football Club is an invitational rugby club open to all players. By tradition at least 1 debutant is selected for each match, and players wear the socks of their home club.

412.   England prop Jason Leonard played 119 times for England and scored 1 try. He also played 6 times for the Barbarians and scored 1 try – against England – thus scoring as many tries against England as for them.

413.   Justin Leonard holed a 45 foot putt in the 1999 Ryder Cup that prompted an American invasion of the putting green before opponent Jose Maria Olazabal had his chance to make his birdie putt. Earlier in the day US Captain Tom Lehmann had also celebrated wildly after holing a putt, prompting Torrance to remark with just a hint of overreaction that "It was disgusting and Tom Lehmann calls himself a man of God. His behaviour today was disgusting".

414.   Although Olazabal missed his birdie putt in 1999, he holds the unofficial record for the longest ever successful putt**, which he holed on the way to the 1999 tournament. With Concorde travelling at 1,270mph, Olazabal successfully putted the length of the cabin into a cup. The putt took 26 seconds, during which time the plane had travelled 9.2 miles.

415.   Christian Marty, the pilot of the Concorde that crashed in Paris in 2000, was the 1st Frenchman to windsurf across the Atlantic, taking 37 days to do it in 1982.

416.   RAF pilot/sportsmen include Donald Findlay, who read the athletes' oath at the 1948 Olympic Games, and England's record rugby union try scorer, Rory Underwood. Underwood scored 49 tries for England and 1 for the British & Irish Lions. Underwood's Lions debut was on the 1989 Australia tour. On that tour teammate Jeremy Guscott debuted for the Lions, despite only having 1 England cap (against Romania). Guscott played in 2 tests on the tour, meaning that for several months he had more caps for the Lions than for his home country. Although many players have played for the British and Irish Lions whilst still uncapped by their own country, this has only happened twice since 1945 – Alun Lewis in 1977 and H John C Brown in 1962. Neither Brown nor Lewis ever played for their country, but in 1968 Brown represented Great Britain in the 4 man bobsleigh competition at the Grenoble Olympics.

417.   Norway topped the medal table at the 1968 Winter Olympics, beating the Soviet Union into second place. In the 9 Winter Olympics that the Soviet Union took part in (from 1956 to 1988), they topped the medal table 7 times, coming second to Norway in 1968 and second to East Germany in 1984.

418.   No Southern Hemisphere city has hosted the Winter Olympics**.

419.   The only Southern Hemisphere cities to host the Summer Olympics are Melbourne, Sydney and Rio de Janeiro**.

420.   6 countries have hosted both Summer and Winter Olympic games : USA (4/4), France (2/3), Canada (1/2), Germany (2/1), Italy (1/2), Japan (1/2)*.

421.   At each of the Summer Olympics from 1924 to 1936 (Paris, Amsterdam, Los Angeles and Berlin), an American athlete that went on to play Tarzan in films won a medal (Johnny Weismuller, Buster Crabbe, Herman Brix and Glenn Morris).

422.   Kareem Abdul-Jabbar, who was NBA MVP 6 times in the 10 years from 1971–1980, played the co-pilot Roger Murdock in *Airplane*, (he is the Roger referred to in the "Roger, Roger, what's our vector, Victor" conversation). No other player has won the MVP as many times** (both Michael Jordan and Bill Russell won it 5 times).

423.   Michael Jordan wore the number 23 for most of his career with the Chicago Bulls, and the shirt number was retired in 1994 after he had retired. When he came out of retirement he had to choose a new number (45) because 23 had been retired. England cricketer Marcus Trescothick's squad number was 23, David Beckham's squad number at Real Madrid was 23, and Shane Warne had 23 for all his professional clubs and for the Australian one day team, all in homage to Jordan.

424.   In 2003 when Cameroonian footballer Marc-Vivien Foe died after suffering a heart attack while

playing in the Federations Cup, his club Manchester City retired his squad number, which was 23.

425.   Manchester City is believed to be the only professional football club in the world to have been founded by a woman, after the pivotal role Anna Connell played in establishing the club.

426.   Manchester City's 1st major honour was the FA Cup, which they won in 1904 against Bolton Wanderers at Crystal Palace. Billy Meredith scored Manchester City's winner in the 1-0 victory. Meredith is the only player to have played over 100 games for both Manchester City and Manchester United**.

427.   Andrew Cole, who played for both Manchester United and Manchester City, is one of 9 players who have scored in the Premier League for 6 or more different clubs**, along with Les Ferdinand, Darren Bent, Marcus Bent, Nick Barmby, Craig Bellamy, Peter Crouch, Nicolas Anelka and Robbie Keane.

428.   Cole's only goal for England came in the same match as Ashley Cole's debut for England, against Albania in 2001, when both A Coles played the whole match together.

429.   When England beat Wales in the 2006 Six Nations Championship, lock Adam Jones came on as a substitute, joining prop Adam Jones and also joining M Jones, D Jones and S Jones on the pitch. Michael Owen (not the footballer) was also playing at the time. Michael Owen the rugby player and Michael Owen the football player both captained their countries in 2005.

430. Phil Neal, Max Woosnam and Peter Beardsley all captained the England football team once.

431. Allan Lamb, David Gower and Marcus Trescothick all ended their careers with 1 test match wicket.

432. 19 players have taken a wicket with their 1st ball in test match cricket**. Maurice Tate took a wicket with his 1st ball in test match cricket, helping England to dismiss South Africa for 30, the lowest ever 1st innings total in a test match**.

433. Shane Warne took Mike Gatting's wicket with his 1st ball against England, in 1993, with the 'Ball of The Century', (he already had 31 test match wickets).

434. Warne never got a century in international cricket. Against New Zealand in a 2001 test match, he was out for 99, caught trying to slog sweep Daniel Vettori.

435. Donald Bradman went into his final test match, against England at the Oval in 1948, with a career average of 101.39. Needing only 4 to maintain a career average above 100.00 (or any not out score to stay above 100.00), Bradman was bowled for a second ball duck by Eric Hollies. Bradman could still have achieved the average in the second innings but he did not bat as Australia won by an innings and 149 runs. Not to be confused with : the 1st ball Bradman received in the Bodyline series, in the second test at Adelaide in 1932/33, when he was bowled by Bill Bowes for a

golden duck, dramatized in the 1984 Australian television mini-series *Bodyline*.

436.   Bradman was one of Wisden's Five Cricketers of the 20th Century, along with Gary Sobers, Shane Warne, Viv Richards and Jack Hobbs.

437.   In the Academy Award winning film *Slumdog Millionaire*, the penultimate question, for 10 million Indian Rupees, is "Which cricketer has scored the most first class centuries in history?" The possible answers are Sachin Tendulkar, Ricky Ponting, Michael Slater and Jack Hobbs, and Jamal correctly guesses Hobbs after using his 50:50 lifeline to narrow the answers to Ponting and Hobbs.

438.   Michael Slater has a tattoo of the number 356, a reference to his Australian test cricket cap number. Unfortunately both Slater and Brendon Julian debuted in the same match, and as the caps are awarded alphabetically when that occurs, Slater was actually 357. However in 2011 the Australian Cricket Board confirmed that as Slater had been told he was 356, and given that Julian didn't mind, Slater could keep the number.

439.   David Beckham's tattoos include the Christian iconography of a guardian angel, a winged cross, an angel with the words 'In the face of adversity', Jesus on the way to the cross, and Jesus rising from the tomb. The devout Christian commented after the birth of his 1st child "I definitely want Brooklyn to be christened, but I don't know into what religion yet".

440.   Brooklyn born and raised Mike Tyson has been a pigeon fancier from a young age, even fronting a TV series *Taking on Tyson* in which he entered competitive pigeon racing.

441.   Live pigeon shooting appeared at the 1900 Olympics. Approximately 300 pigeons were killed, in the only Olympic event where animals were intentionally killed. At the opening ceremony of the 1988 Seoul Olympic Games, several doves who had been released during the ceremony and were perching on the cauldron, were burnt alive when the Olympic flame was lit. Releasing doves first occurred in an Olympic opening ceremony at the 1st games after World War One in Antwerp in 1920.

442.   The Antwerp Olympics was also the 1st where the Olympic athletes' oath was taken. The oath was : "We swear we will take part in the Olympic Games in a spirit of chivalry, for the honour of our country and for the glory of sport". It now reads "In the name of all the competitors I promise that we shall take part in these Olympic Games, respecting and abiding by the rules which govern them, committing ourselves to a sport without doping and without drugs, in the true spirit of sportsmanship, for the glory of sport and the honour of our teams" although foreign translations have been used.

443.   The Antwerp Olympics featured the only Olympic event to ever have been contested in 2 countries**. The 1st race in the 12' dinghy competition took place in Belgium and last 2 races were held in the Netherlands.

444.   Belgium is the smallest country (by area) to have hosted the Summer Olympics**.

445.   Famous Belgian sportsmen include Olympic gold medal tennis player Justine Henin, Kim Clijsters, 5 time Tour de France winners Eddy Merckx, and footballer Jean-Marc Bosman. When Bosman's contract with RFC Liege expired in 1990, he wanted to move to Dunkerque but they refused to pay the transfer fee demanded by Liege. The Bosman Ruling allowed players to transfer for free after their contract has expired.

446.   The European Court also found in favour of a sportsman when Slovenian handball player Marius Kolpak argued for his right to play in the European Union. The ruling has a profound impact in cricket, where Kolpak became a term to describe a foreign player (especially South African) who held an EU passport and therefore did not count towards a team's quota of foreign players.

447.   Between 1968 and 1992 Yorkshire County Cricket Club only selected players who were born within the historic boundaries of Yorkshire (later extended to include where a player was educated). When the rule was relaxed the 1st non-Yorkshireman to be selected was Sachin Tendulkar.

448.   Athletic Club Bilbao has a policy of selecting Basques or players with direct Basque ancestry. The club's shirts are modelled on Southampton FC's strip, and it was not until 2008 that the club shirts bore the name of a commercial sponsor.

449.   In 1976 Kettering Town became the 1st British team to wear a shirt sponsor, Kettering Tyres. The FA ordered them to remove the name, and the club changed it to Kettering T, claiming this stood for Kettering Town, which the FA rejected.

450.   Non-league Kettering Town have scored more goals in the history of the FA Cup than any other club**.

451.   The most recent time a non-league team beat a top division team in the FA Cup** was in January 2013 when Luton Town beat Norwich City 1-0. 24 years earlier Norwich ended the FA Cup run of the previous team to beat a top flight team in the Cup, thrashing Sutton United 8-0 after Sutton had beaten top flight Coventry City 2-1. Coventry City had won the competition 2 years earlier in 1986/87.

452.   Coventry City's badge, and the civic emblem of the city itself, has an elephant on it.

453.   The Ivory Coast national football team's nickname is The Elephants.

454.   The Elephants were scheduled to play Togo in the 2010 African Cup of Nations. Togo withdrew following a gun attack on their team bus, in which 3 people were killed, on their way to their base 2 days before the tournament's 1st game. Showing great sensitivity to their plight, the Confederation of African Football disqualified Togo, fined them $50,000 and banned them from the next 2 tournaments.

455.   Chile's football team, known as La Roja, were disqualified from the 1990 and 1994 FIFA World Cups after the Roberto Rojas Scandal. During a 1989 qualifying match against Brazil, when a defeat would have eliminated Chile, they were 1-0 down when goalkeeper Rojas fell to the ground clutching his head with a firework thrown from the crowd nearby. Rojas was carried off and the match was abandoned after Chile refused to play on. Video footage showed the firework had not hit Rojas, the match awarded to Brazil, and Chile banned for 2 tournaments.

456.   The Soviet Union were disqualified from the 1974 World Cup after refusing to play Chile following the 1973 coup d'etat by Augusto Pinochet. The lack of opponents didn't deter Chile from starting the match in front of spectators, passing the ball into an empty net to take an unassailable 1-0 aggregate lead.

457.   Tim Henman was the 1st player in the Open era to be disqualified from Wimbledon, after hitting a ball into a ball girl during a doubles match in 1995. One of Henman and partner Jeremy Bates' opponents that day was Jeff Tarango. 3 days after Henman's disqualification, Tarango became the second player to be defaulted at Wimbledon after storming off court, having been a point penalty for swearing at the crowd and telling the umpire he was "the most corrupt official in the game".

458.   Henman's great grandmother, Ellen Stanwell-Brown, was the 1st woman to serve overarm at Wimbledon, in 1901.

459. Henman Hill at Wimbledon, where spectators can watch a giant video screen, is officially known as Aorangi Terrace.

460. The hill at Lord's cricket ground is approximately 8 feet, rising from the south east to the north west.

461. Extreme 19th is a 400m par 3 hole on the Legend Golf and Safari Resort in South Africa. The tee is 430m above the green and is accessible only by helicopter, and the green is not only shaped like Africa but also has contours representing Africa's mountains. Padraig Harrington was the 1st person to par the hole.

462. The longest par 3 in major golf is the 288 yard par 3 8th hole at Oakmont Country Club in Pennsylvania**. Oakmont has hosted the US Open more than any other course (8 times)**. Southern Hills Country Club has held the most USPGA Championship (4)**, Augusta National has held every Masters Tournament, and St Andrews has hosted The Open Championship most times (29)*.

463. The Open Championship has only been held outside England or Scotland once**, in 1951 at Royal Portrush Golf Club in Northern Ireland.

464. Only 4 Northern Irishmen have won majors**. After Fred Daly's Open Championship win in 1947, there was a 63 year wait, and then Graeme McDowell, Rory McIlroy and Darren Clarke won 4 out of the next 11 tournaments.

465.   When Clarke won the Open Championship in 2010, after McIlroy had won the US Open tournament before, it was the 1st time since 1910 that 2 different golfers from 1 country, other than the United States, had won consecutive majors.

466.   McIlroy was engaged to marry tennis player Caroline Wozniacki. Wozniacki became world number 1 in 2010, but has never won a grand slam tournament**. Since the WTA rankings began in 1975 only 2 other players have reached number 1 without winning a grand slam tournament : Jelena Jankovic and Dinara Safina**. The only man to have achieved this feat is Marcelo Rios**.

467.   A tennis net is 3 feet 6 inches high at the net posts and 3 feet high in the middle.

468.   A real tennis net is 5 feet high at the net posts and 3 feet high in the middle.

469.   Jim Dear was an Englishman who won the British Open squash tournament in 1939 when it was the de facto World Championship, was world champion of rackets between 1947 and 1954, and world champion of real tennis from 1955 to 1957.

470.   There was a rackets court on RMS Titanic.

471.   Although badminton is technically the fastest racket sport in the world, with the shuttlecock reaching speeds of 200mph immediately after it is hit, the ball in rackets travels at up to 170mph and does not

decelerate as quickly as a shuttlecock. In squash the ball can travel at approximately 125mph.

472.   The coloured dot on a squash ball indicates its bounciness. From slowest to fastest, the colours are orange, double yellow, yellow, green, white, red and blue. Competition standard is double yellow, although some high altitude venues use orange.

473.   Orange balls are used in the World Ice Golf Championships held at Uummannaq in Greenland. The annual 36 hole tournament is held over 2 days in March when the average temperature is -14 degrees centigrade.

474.   The 2 most famous long distance dog sled races are the Yukon Quest (from Fairbanks, Alaska to Whitehorse, Yukon) and the Iditarod (from Anchorage, Alaska to Nome, Alaska).

475.   The colour scheme for greyhounds racing in Great Britain is red jacket with white numeral 1, blue with white numeral 2, white with black numeral 3, black with white numeral 4, orange with black numeral 5, black and white stripes with red numeral 6.

476.   The most prestigious race in British greyhound racing is the English Greyhound Derby, raced at White City (originally built for the 1908 Olympics) until its demolition in 1985, and subsequently held at Wimbledon Stadium. The stuffed body of Mick the Miller, 1 of only 4 dogs to have won the Derby more than once, is on display at the Natural History Museum at Tring in Hertfordshire.

477.   Mick Mills is the only England captain who has captained England at World Cups and never lost a game**. Mills captained England during the 1982 World Cup when England were eliminated despite being undefeated. Although Bobby Moore was undefeated in 1966, he captained the team that lost to Brazil and West Germany in 1970.

478.   Moore and Billy Wright share the record for the most number of times they have captained England** : 90 times each. Wright is the only captain to have captained England in 3 World Cup finals** (1950, 1954 and 1958). Diego Maradona of Argentina holds the record for most World Cup finals matches as captain with 16**.

479.   The player that Maradona beat twice during his dribble to score the Goal of the Century against England in the quarter final of the 1986 World Cup was Terry Butcher.

480.   Terry Butcher managed Scottish football club Inverness Caledonian Thistle between 2009 and 2013. The 1st manager of the club, after the merger or Caledonian and Inverness Thistle, was Sergei Baltacha, who played for the Soviet Union in the 1988 European Championship Final when Marco van Basten of the Netherlands scored a volley, regarded by many as the greatest ever goal in a major final. Baltacha is the father of former British number 1 tennis player Elena Baltacha.

481.   British tennis player Anne Keothavong's parents are from Laos. No one representing Laos has ever won

an Olympic medal**. Monaco has attended most games without winning a medal**.

482.   Albert II, Prince of Monaco, competed for Monaco in bobsled at all 5 Olympics from 1988 to 2002, with a highest ever finish of 24th. Prince Albert is married to South African Charlene Wittstock, who competed in swimming at the 2000 Sydney Olympics.

483.   Other famous Olympians include General Patton (pentathlon in 1912), Princess Anne (equestrianism in 1976) and her daughter Zara Phillips (equestrianism silver medallist in 2012], baby doctor Benjamin Spock (rowing gold medallist in 1924), and violinist Vanessa-Mae who was subsequently banned from competition for 4 years due to irregularities in the qualifying events.

484.   Princess Anne won the BBC Sports Personality of the Year award in 1971, and her daughter Zara Philips won it in 2006. Philips' husband, Mike Tindall, won the Team of the Year award in 2003 as part of the England squad that won the rugby union World Cup that year.

485.   The only snooker player to have won the individual Award is Steve Davis in 1988**.

486.   In 1969, naturalist David Attenborough was the Controller of BBC2 when the channel commissioned the snooker show *Pot Black* in order to utilise the new colour technology.

487.   In 1991-92, Channel 4 broadcast a programme on the Asian sport of kabaddi. In this sport teams try to win points by entering into opposition territory, during

which attempts they must hold 1 breath and chant 'kabaddi' repeatedly. India have won all 4 World Cups held since the inaugural tournament in 2004.

488.   Gary Imlach, co-host of Channel 4's coverage of American football and the Tour de France, won the William Hill Sports Book of the Year award for his biography of his father, a professional footballer in the 1950s and 1960s. Stewart Imlach scored the 1st goal against Manchester United after the 1958 Munich Air Disaster that killed 23 people.

489.   When Manchester United beat Bayern Munich in 1999 to win their second European Cup/Champions League trophy, their goals were in the 91st and 93rd minutes. David Beckham and Gary Neville both played in that game, and also played in the 2004 European Championship group game when England, leading 1-0 at 90 minutes, conceded 2 goals from Zinedine Zidane in the 91st and 93rd minutes (a free kick and a penalty). Beckham had missed a penalty in the game, and went on to miss another penalty in the unsuccessful shoot out against Portugal in the quarter final.

490.   Both of Zidane's parents emigrated from Algeria to France. The Algerian philosopher and novelist Albert Camus, winner of the Nobel Prize for Literature in 1957, is often wrongly credited as having played in goal for Algeria. He did however play in goal for the junior team of Racing Universitaire d'Alger, a successful North African club.

491.   3 goalkeepers have captained a World Cup winning team : Gianpiero Combi, Dino Zoff and Iker Casillas**.

492.   England's World Cup winning goalkeeper Gordon Banks lost the sight in his right eye after a car accident in 1972. He played 8 more times for Stoke City before retiring from English football.

493.   5 goalkeepers have scored in the Premier League, all from open play** : Peter Schmeichel, Brad Friedel, Tim Howard, Paul Robinson, and Asmir Begovic. Schmeichel scored for Aston Villa.

494.   Argentinian footballer Ricky Villa had joined Tottenham after the 1978 World Cup, along with fellow Argentinian Ossie Ardiles. During his time at Tottenham, in 1981, Ardiles appeared in *Escape to Victory*, a film about a football match in a Prisoner of War camp in World War Two. In the match that is the denouement of the film, the Allies draw 4-4 with the Germans, with goals from Bobby Moore, Ossie Ardiles, Polish international Kazimierz Deyna and Pele.

495.   At the 1982 World Cup Finals, Ardiles wore the Argentinian number 1 shirt as their squad were numbered alphabetically, with the only exception being that Diego Maradona was given his preferred number 10. The only other outfield player to have worn 1 at a World Cup Finals is Argentina's Norberto Alonso in 1978. Other players allocated squad number 1 (Netherlands' Ruud Geels in 1974 and Argentina's Sergio Almiron in 1986) did not play. In 1974 Johann Cruyff was alphabetically 1st but chose to wear his

favoured number 14 instead, so Geels was allocated 1. Since the 2010 tournament, FIFA have insisted that number 1 be assigned to a goalkeeper. When Alonso wore 1, Ardiles wore 2.

496.   Ferdinand Alonso is the only Spaniard to have become Formula One World Drivers Champion**, having won consecutively in 2005 and 2006. Only 9 other drivers have won twice in a row**, including Juan Manuel Fangio (won 4 times in a row), and Michael Schumacher (5 times in a row from 2000 to 2004, all 5 wins with Ferrari).

497.   Ferrari's logo is a prancing horse, known as Cavallino Rampante. In 1923 Enzo Ferrari met the mother of Italian World War One ace fighter pilot Count Francesco Baracco, who had a horse painted on his planes. Ferrari's prancing horse is different in several respects to Baracca's, but has been used officially by Ferrari since 1929.

498.   Le Stade de Roland Garros, where the French Open tennis tournament is played, is named after World War One ace fighter pilot Roland Garros. Garros was responsible for inventing the 1st successful forward firing airplane machine gun, synchronising the timing of the firing so that bullets passed through the rotating propeller.

499.   The last Frenchman to win the French Open Men's Singles was Yannick Noah in 1983**. The most recent home grown winners of the singles tournaments at each of the grand slam tournaments are

Australian Open** : Mark Edmondson (1976) and Chris O'Neil (1978)

French Open** : Yannick Noah (1983) and Mary Pierce (2000)

Wimbledon** : Andy Murray (2013) and Virginia Wade (1977)

US Open** : Andy Roddick (2003) and Serena Williams (2014)

500.   The FIFA World Cup has been won by the host nation 6 times** : 1930 (Uruguay), 1934 (Italy), 1966 (England), 1974 (West Germany), 1978 (Argentina) and 1998 (France).

Part 2

Football

1. Which 3 of England's 1966 FIFA World Cup winners have since been knighted? (30)
2. Which footballer has played for 3 countries at the FIFA World Cup finals? (74)
3. Which 3 countries have won every FIFA World Cup Final they have appeared in? (75)
4. Which 4 countries have lost every FIFA World Cup Final they have appeared in? (75)
5. Which 11 teams in the Football League have nicknames that do not end in the letter 's'? (83)
6. What were the 12 original Football League members? (84)
7. Which teams have the shortest and longest names in the Football League (excluding spaces between words and the words 'association', 'football' or 'club')? (85)
8. Which 6 British football teams have won the European Cup/Champions League? (128)
9. Which 8 post-war England footballers have an 'x' in their surname? (173)
10. Which 9 cities have provided more than 1 European Cup/Champions League semi finalist? (208)
11. Which 3 substitutes have scored 2 goals in an FA Cup Final? (314)
12. Which 2 grounds have hosted both a test match and an FA Cup Final? (315)

13. Which 6 players have won the Premier League with more than 1 club? (346)
14. Which player has won the FIFA World Cup, the UEFA European Championships, the Champions League, the Premier League and the FA Cup? (347)
15. Which 9 players have scored in the Premier League for 6 or more clubs? (427)
16. Who is the only England captain to have never lost a match at the FIFA World Cup finals? (477)
17. Which 5 goalkeepers have scored in the Premier League? (493)
18. How many times has the host country won the FIFA World Cup? (500)

Cricket

19. Who holds the record for the most career wickets in test matches? (39)
20. Which 4 batsmen have hit 6 sixes in an over in international or first class cricket? (106)
21. Name the 11 ways in which a batsman can be dismissed in cricket. (115)
22. Who were Wisden's 5 Cricketers of the 20th Century? (436)

Tennis

23. Which 4 current players (2 men, 2 women) have won career Grand Slams (all 4 grand slam singles tournaments during their career)? (14)

24. Which 4 players (2 men, 3 women) have won the Grand Slam (all four singles tournaments in one season)? (15)
25. Which current player has won 3 of the 4 grand slam singles tournaments, and which one is he or she missing? (14)
26. Who are the most recent home grown winners of the singles tournaments at each of the 4 grand slam tournaments? (499)

Golf

27. Which 5 golfers have won all 4 major tournaments during the career? (7)
28. Which 2 current players have won 3 of the 4 major tournaments, and which one are each of them missing? (7)
29. Which 9 courses are currently on the Open Championship rota? (51)
30. Which 7 golfers have held the world number 1 ranking since 1st January 2000? (69)
31. Golfers from how many different countries have represented Europe at the Ryder Cup? (72)

Athletics

32. How many Olympic Games have been cancelled? (36)
33. How many athletes have won medals at both the Summer and Winter Olympic Games? (37)
34. Which 10 events comprise the decathlon? (46)

35. Which 3 sportsmen have successfully defended their Olympic titles in 3 successive games, in individual sports? (219)
36. Which 3 people have opened more than 1 Olympic Games? (360)
37. What is the most recent host country to have won no gold medals at its own Summer Olympics? (361)
38. What is the most recent host country to have won no gold medals at its own Winter Olympics? (362)
39. Which 3 Southern Hemisphere cities have hosted the Summer Olympics? (419)
40. Which 6 countries have hosted both the Summer and Winter Olympics? (420)
41. What is the smallest country to have hosted the Summer Olympics? (444)

Mixed Bag

42. Which 3 races comprise the Triple Crown in American horseracing? (19)
43. Which 4 snooker player from outside the UK have won the World Snooker Championship? (25)
44. Who is the only sportsman to have won Olympic gold medals in different sports at the Winter and Summer Olympics? (37)
45. Which 4 sportsmen have won the BBS Overseas Sports Personality of the Year more than once? (57)
46. Which 4 cyclists have won the Tour de France 5 times? (77)

47. Name the 10 British Formula 1 World Champion Drivers. (103)
48. What are the 5 Classics of British horseracing? (169)
49. Which 4 players have played in both Rugby Union and Rugby League World Cup Finals? (213)
50. Which 4 players have won the Rugby Union World Cup twice? (214)

Index

A

America's Cup : origin 196; trophy vandalised 197

Amiss, Dennis 304

Anderson, Viv 129

Anelka, Nicolas : international record 346; Premier League goals 427

Anmer 12

Anquetil, Jacques 77

Aorangi Terrace 459

Archer, Jeffrey 389

Archery : scoring 62; etymology 389

Ardiles, Osvaldo : *Escape to Victory* 494; 1982 World Cup shirt number 495

Armstrong, Lance 77

Ashes cricket : honours for 2005 winners 29; Bodyline Series 150; Centenary Test Match 154; 1981 Headingley 226; series batting average over 100 287; Gary Pratt run out 333; domination by 1 team 392; Compton-Miller medal 393

Aston Villa : European Cup victory 128; name 207

Athletic Club Bilbao 448

Athletics world records : longest standing 89; indoor/outdoor records 91; maximum windspeed/altitude 96; Ethiopia's record 320; steeplechase jumps 321

Attapattu, Marvan : retired out 117; most ducks in test matches 338

Attenborough, David 486

Augusta National Golf Club female members 158; racism 285; host of the Masters Tournament 462

Australian Open (tennis) : trophies 264; most recent victories by Australians 499

B

Babe Ruth : name 8; Curse of The Bambino 9; nicknames 388

Badminton : shuttlecock 1; origins 2; speed 471

Badminton Horse Trials 2

Badminton House 2

Bafana Bafana 281

Balderstone, Chris 104

Ball of the Century 433

Ballesteros, Severiano 284

Baltacha, Elena 480

Baltacha, Sergei 480

Baltimore Orioles 388

Banks, Gordon 492

Bannister, Roger 222

Banyana Banyana 281

Barbarians Football Club 411

Barcelona (song) 359

Baresi, Franco 327

Barmby, Nick : move from Everton to Liverpool 349; England goals 350; association with Hull 351; Premier League goals 427

Barton, Joey 271

Baseball : dimensions 246; origin of southpaw 340

Basketball : invention 4; climax of 1972 Olympic Games final and USA record at Olympic Games 355

Battiston, Patrick 204

Battle of Santiago 68

Battledore and shuttlecock 2

Baze, Russell 204

BBC Sports Personality of The Year/Overseas Sports Personality of The Year : cricketer winners 56; overseas winners 57; first winner 222; Princess Anne, Zara Phillips and Mike Tindall victories 484; only snooker player winner 485

BBC theme tunes 248

Beamon, Bob 95

Beardsley, Peter : move from Liverpool to Everton 349; England captain 430

Beckham, David : Spice Boys 325; shirt number at Real Madrid 423; tattoos 439; 1999 Champions League victory and defeat to France at 2004 European Championship 489

Beckham, Victoria 326

Begovic, Azmir 493

Behr, Karl 13

Belgian sportsmen 445

Bellamy, Craig 427

Belmont Stakes 19

Belov, Sergei 355

Bena Tshadi 263

Bent, Darren 427

Bent, Marcus 427

Berg, Henning 346

Bergomi, Giuseppe 327

Bermuda : cricket 282; PGA Grand Slam of Golf 283

Best, George 252

Betjeman, John 235

Biathlon 46

Bikila, Abebe 320
Billie the horse 255
Black Caps 81
Blair, Tony 293
Blissett, Gary 270
Blissett, Luther : Watford player 268; anarchists 269
Blue 133
Boateng, Jerome 406
Boateng, Kevin-Prince 406
Boggs, Wade 187
Bogues, Muggsy 379
Bohr, Harald 382
Bohr, Niels 382
Bol, Manute 379
Bolt, Usain 57
Bonds, Barry 192
Bonds, Bobby 192
Borg, Bjorn 230
Borotra, Jean 265
Bosman ruling 445
Bosman, Jean Marc 445
Boston Celtics 125
Boston Red Sox : record in World Series 9; name 179; ownership 180
Boston United 178
Botham, Ian : BBC Sports Personality of the Year 56; father and son sportsmen 192; 1981 Headingley 226; professional football 227
Botham, Liam 192
Bowls : Sir Francis Drake 399; equipment 400
Bowyer, Lee 272

Boycott, Geoffrey : first one day international match 155; rebel tour to South Africa 304

Boycotts 156

Bradford City fire 227

Bradman, Donald : Bodyline Series and career average 150; final test match duck 435; Wisden Cricketers of the Century 436

Brady, Tom 118

Bramall Lane 315

Brazil, Alan 32

Bristow, Eric 110

British & Irish Lions : 99 call 147; Battle of Boet Erasmus 148; players not capped for country 416

British Open (see Open Championship)

Brix, Herman 421

Broad, Chris : father and son sportsmen 192; attack on Sri Lanka team in 2009 337

Broad, Stuart : father and son 192; hat trick 262

Brown, Gordon (British Prime Minister) 148

Brown, Gordon (rugby union player) 148

Brown, John C 416

Brugnon, Jacques 265

Bruno, Frank 313

Bryan, Bob : career titles 138; twins 217

Bryan, Mike 217

Bubka, Sergei 90

Budd, Zola 303

Budge, Don 14

Butcher, Terry : Goal of the Century 478; managerial career 479

C

Caballe, Montserrat 359
Cabrera, Angel 7
Campbell, Donald 191
Campbell, Malcolm 191
Campbell, Menzies 222
Camus, Albert 490
Carbajal, Antonio 164
Carnoustie Golf Links : 1953 Open Championship 7;
Open Championship rota 51
Carroll, Lewis 131
Carter, Ali 242
Cartwright, Alexander 245
Casillas, Iker 491
Cech, Petr 32
Celtic : Scottish Football Championships 127; European
Cup victory 128; name 207; nickname 389
Chamberlain, Neville (politician) 23
Chamberlain, Neville (soldier) 23
Champions League (see under European Cup)
Chappell, Trevor 40
Chariots of Fire : story 53; Best Picture Oscar 180
Charlton Athletic : name 207; nickname 389
Charlton, Bobby : knighthood 30 ; clubs played for 31;
1968 European Cup Final 251
Charlton, Jack : club not played for 31; club played for
327
Chataway, Chris 222

D

Davis, Fred 25

Davis, George 396, 397

Davis, Steve : Black Ball Final 240; televised 147 break 241; BBC Sports Personality of the Year 485

Davison, Emily 12

de Boer, Frank 217

de Boer, Ronald 217

de Pourtales, Helene 34

Dear, Jim 469

Deaths 263

Decathlon : events 46 ; world record 47

Decker, Mary 303

Derby Stakes (The Derby) : disqualified winner 11; Suffragette death 12; Lester Piggott career record 170

Devon Loch : fall in Grand National 240; Dick Francis 300

Deyna, Kazimierz 494

di Stefano, Alfredo : international caps 74; European Cup Final hat trick 250; FIFA World Cup 252

Didrickson, Mildred (Babe) 48

Ding Junhui 25

Dixon, Kerry 173

Dixon, Lee 173

Djokovic, Novak 14

Dodd, Lottie 63

Dog sled racing 474

Doherty, Ken 25

Donald, Luke 189

Drake, Francis 399

du Randt, Os : multiple World Cup winner 214; name 215

Duel in the Sun 68

E

European Cup/Champions League : British victories 128; cities that have provided 2 semi finalists 208; hat trick in Final 250; hat tricks for more than 1 club 261; most final appearances 328

Evert, Chris : career grand slam 14; marriages 137

F

FA Cup : White Horse Final 255; 2 goals in final by substitutes 314; first final 315; grounds that have hosted FA Cup Final and test match 315; giant killings 451

Faldo, Nick : Masters Tournament Champions Dinner 189; Masters Tournament victory 240, 284

Fangio, Juan Manuel 496

Farrell, Andy 192

Farrell, Owen 192

Fastnet race : Simon Le Bon 397; 1979 disaster 398

Federer, Roger : career grand slam 14 ; BBC Overseas Sports Personality of the Year 57; record between 2004-2011 309

Fenix Two 278

Ferdinand Les : Newcastle United number 9 shirt 293; Premier League goals 427

Ferguson, Duncan 271

Ferrari 497

Field hockey 64

Field of Dreams 258

Formula 1 : British world champions 103; father and son world champions 192; BBC theme tune 247; points system 292; consecutive wins 496

Four Musketeers 265

Fowler, Robbie : cocaine goal celebration 323; asked referee not to give penalty 324; Spice Boys 325

Fox, Don 240

Francis, Dick 300

Francisco, Silvino 172

French Open (tennis) : trophies 264; stadium 498; last French winners 499

Friedel, Brad 493

Fry, C B : all round sportsman 104; view on penalties 166

Fucka, Gregor 260

Furlong, Paul 344

G

Gabba 394

Gallacher, Hughie 293

Garros, Roland 498

Gascoigne, Paul : flute playing celebration 279; dentist's chair celebration 322

Gatting, Mike 433

George Hotel 368

Gerulaitis, Vitas 263

Gibbs, Herschelle 106

Giggs, Ryan 252

Gold Cup (polo) 194

Golden Slam (tennis) 15

H

I

Keegan, Kevin : European Footballer of the Year 295; interview rant against Alex Ferguson 296

Kentucky Derby 19

Keothavong, Anne 480

Kerrigan, Nancy 181

Kettering Town : shirt sponsorship 449; FA Cup goals record 450

Khan, Jahengir 79

Khan, Mansoor Ali 149

Khan, Zaheer 125

Kidd, Brian 251

Kilmarnock 207

King, Bille Jean : career grand slam 14 ; Battle of the Sexes 68

Knickerbocker Rules 245

Knott, Alan 304

Kolpak players 446

Kolpak, Marius 446

Korfball 76

Kratochvilova, Jarmila 89

Krone, Julie 144

Kubala, Laszlo 74

Kumble, Anil 125

L

LA Lakers : name 125; NBA Championships 126

Lacoste, Rene 265

Lacrosse 363

Laker, Jim : BBC Sports Personality of the Year 56; 10 wickets in an innings 125

Lindrum, Horace 25

Liston, Sonny : name 8; 1964 and 1965 vs Muhammad Ali

Little, Jason 214

Liverpool : European Cup victories 128; ownership and club anthem 180; name 207; Heysel Stadium disaster 227

Lloyd, David 231

Lloyd, John 137

Lofthouse, Nat 327

Lord's : test matches hosted 120; name 121; sculpture 122; Sachin Tendulkar's record 123; hit over the pavillion 286; slope 460

Luding, Christa 37

M

MacArthur, Ellen 27

Maccabeus 11

Macdonald, Malcolm 293

Macgill, Stuart 38

Maiden (cricket) 142

Maiden (horseracing) 142

Major Soccer League 348

Maldini, Paolo : 1 club player 327; European Cup Final appearances record 328

Man of Steel 55

Manchester City : founding 425; Billy Meredith 426

Manchester United : European Cup victories 128; first European Cup victory 251; Billy Meredith 426; 1999 Champions League victory 489

Mansell, Nigel 211

Maradona, Diego : Hand of God goal 204; goal celebration at 1994 World Cup and subsequent ban 323; captaincy record 478; Goal of the Century 479; shirt number 495

Marching Song 278

Marsh, Terry 389

Masters Tournament : host club 158; name 159; Champions Dinner 189; par 3 tournament 190; British winners 284; racism 285

Mata, Juan 347

Match of the Day 249

Materazzi, Marco 165

Matthaeus, Lothar 164

Matthews, Jimmy 262

Matthews, Stanley 372

Mazzola, Valentino 252

McAteer, Jason 324, 325

McBride, Willie John 147

McCall, Oliver 313

McCall, Stuart 314

McDowell, Graeme 464

McEnroe, John : Wimbledon debut 229; "You cannot be serious!" 230

McGee, Frank 149

McGrath, Glenn : test match wickets and ducks 125; first T20 international match 332

McIlroy, Rory : major victories 7, 464, 465; Caroline Wozniacki 466

McKay, Heather 78

McManaman, Steve : dentist's chair celebration 322; Spice Boys 325

McNeill, Billy 327

Melbourne Cricket Ground : capacity 43 ; 1956 Olympic Games 44

Mercury, Freddie 359

Mercx, Eddie : Tour de France victories 77; famous Belgian 445

Meredith, Billy 426

Metsu, Bruno 364

Miami Vice 175

Mick the Miller 476

Mickelson, Phil 7

Midwinter, Billy 152

Mikkola, Hannu 210

Milburn, Colin 149

Milburn, Jackie 293

Million Dollar Baby 180

Mills, Mick 476

Milutinovic, Bora 364

Ming, Yao 379

Minnesota Twins 217

Mintonette 3

Modern pentathlon 45

Mohammad, Hanif 107

Monaco : Olympic Games record 481; Prince Albert II at Olympic Games 482

Montana, Joe 118

Montgomerie, Colin 405

Moore, Bobby : OBE 30; name 31; World Cup record 477; England captain 478; *Escape To Victory* 494

Morgan, Eoin 335
Morgan, Morgan 24
Morgan, William G. 3
Morris, Glenn 421
Moses, Ed 161
Mosley, Oswald 389
Mottram, Christopher (Buster) 389
Moynihan, Colin 389
Mr Frisk 87
Muirfield 51
Mulcaire, Glenn 160
Muralitharan, Muttiah : test match wickets 39; test
match ducks 125
Murray, Andy 499
Moussambani, Eric 'The Eel' 88

N

Nadal, Rafael : career grand slam 14; record between
2004-2011 309
Naismith, James 4
National Basketball Association (NBA) : rules 5; tallest
and shortest players 379; MVP records 422
Navratilova, Martina : career grand slam 14; grand slam
titles 138; record between 1982-1986 308
Neal, Phil : Liverpool captain at Heysel Stadium disaster
227; England captain 430
Neale, Phil 227
Neptunes Collonges 256
Neville, Gary 24
Neville, Neville 24

O

Oakmont Country Club 462
Oerter, Al 219
Offiah, Martin 54
Olazabal, Jose Maria : Masters Champions Dinner 189; 199 USA invasion of green 413; longest ever putt 414
Old Course, St Andrews 51, 52
Old, Chris 304
Olympic Games : 1908 venue change 35 ; numbering convention 36; boycotts and ever present countries 156; Great Britain gold medals at Winter Olympics 162; Summer Olympics host cities 182, 419, 444; 1988 100m final; theft of first Olympic flag 198; defended title 3 times 219; medals 257; motto 267; discontinued sports 339; people that have opened 2 games 360; host nation failure to win a gold medal 361, 362; opening parade 380; football at the Olympic Games 381, 382; Winter Olympics medal tables 417; Winter Olympics host cities 418; countries to host both Summer and Winter Olympics 420; doves killed in opening ceremony 441; athletes' oath 442; event staged in 2 countries 443; most appearances with no medal 481
On Her Majesty's Secret Service 307
O'Neill, Chris 499
Onischenko, Boris 45
Open Championship : victory in only appearance 7 ; rota of courses 51 ; Duel in the Sun 68; name 159; Jean Van de Velde collapse 239; Tiger Woods strategy at 2006 Open Championship 401; held outside of England and Scotland 463
O'Sullevan, Peter 300

P

Q

R

Robidoux, Alain 298
Robinson, Jackie 130
Robinson, Jason 213
Robinson, Paul 493
Rocky 180
Roddick, Andy 499
Rogers, Mat 213
Roma 319
Rose Bowl (Hampshire) 120
Rose Bowl (Pasadena) 120
Royal Birkdale 51
Royal Liverpool (Hoylake) 51
Royal Lytham & St Anne's 51
Royal Portrush 463
Royal St George's 50, 51
Royal Troon 51
Rugby League : appeared in Union and League World Cup Finals 213; origins 368
Rugby League World Cup : theft of trophy 367; Australia's record 369
Rugby Union : origins 202; Nick Beal/Neil Back anagram and England's biggest victory 212; appeared in Union and League World Cup Finals 213; multiple World Cup winning players 214; game ending 0-0 331; New Zealand record against Scotland 331; longest winning streak 356
Rugby Union World Cup : honours for 2003 winners 28; players sent off 146; Will Greenwood shirt number 186; climax of 2003 Final 297; Australia's record 366
Rumble in the Jungle 68
Running Rein 11
Rusedski, Greg 311

Rush, Ian : World Cup record 252; 2 goals in FA Cup final 314

Ryder Cup : War on the Shore 68 ; postponed due to 9/11 70 ; participation by Europeans 71, 72; Colin Montgomerie's record 405; brothers in team 405; 1999 USA invasion of green 413

S

Shastri, Ravi 106

Shaw, Simon 28

Shearer, Alan : Newcastle number 9 293; England penalties 310; dentist's chair goal celebration 322

Sheedy, Kevin 349

Sheffield Wednesday 389

Shergar 170

Sheringham, Teddy 373

Shoemaker, Willie 204

Shorter, Frank 266

Shriver, Pam 307

Sidebottom, Arnie 304

Silva, David 347

Simpson, O.J. : robbery and kidnap 172; tax evasion 289

Singh, Harbhajan : 39, 125

Singh, Vijay : major victories 7; allegations of cheating 403; major victories 404

Singh, Yuvraj 106

Six Nations Championship : history 17; Wales field 5 players called Jones 429

Slater, Michael : *Slumdog Millionaire* 437; tattoo mistake 438

Slumdog Millionaire 436

Sobers, Garfield : 6 sixes in an over 106; highest test match score 107

Socrates 409

Song, Rigobert 164

Sorenstam, Annika 49

Souness, Graeme 272

Southpaw 340

Sphairistike (see under Tennis)

Sports Personality of The Year (see BBC Sports Personality of The Year)
Squash : speed 471; balls 472
St Lawrence cricket ground, Canterbury 374
Stankovic, Dejan 74
Stanley Cup 371
Steele, David 56
Stewart, Payne 263
Stewart, Ray 184
Stubbins, Albert 59
Sukur, Hakan 273
Sunderland 82
Sunderland, Alan 32
Superbowl : Most Valuable Player award 118; name 119; winners' rings 276
Superstitions 187
Surtees, John 104
Sutton United 451
Swimming The Channel 235

T

T20 cricket 332
Table tennis : Fred Perry 112; longest rally 113
Tall Blacks 81
Tamms, Jacob Tullin 37
Tarango, Jeff 457
Tarzan 421
Tate, Maurice 431
Taylor, Dennis 240
Taylor, Graham 268

Taylor, Les 304

Taylor, Phil 110

Tendulkar, Sachin : record at Lord's 123; *Slumdog Millionaire* 437; first overseas player for Yorkshire 447

Tennis : definition of Open Era 16; origin 139; world rankings 466; net height 467

Tevez, Carlos 346

The Hustler 216

The Lamb 256

The Postage Stamp 237

Thomas, Clive 204

Thomas, Mickey 172

Thorburn, Cliff : snooker World Champion 25; maximum break 241

Thorpe, Jim 48

Tikhonov, Alexander 219

Tin Cup 258

Tindall, Mike 483

Togo 454

Torres, Fernando 347

Torvill & Dean 182

Tour de France : jersey colours 41 ; winners 78

Toure, Kolo : superstition 187; Premier League winner with more than 1 club 346

Trescothick, Marcus : shirt number 423; test match wickets 431

Triathlon : format 46; terminology 233; Ironman 234

Trickle, Dick 260

Triple Crown (horseracing) : definition 19; female winner 144

Triple Crown (rugby union) 18

Trott, Albert 286
Trott, Jonathan 287
Troussier, Philippe 364
Trumble, Hugh 262
Tug o' War 339
Turnberry Resort : Open Championship rota 51; venue
for Open Championships 136
Twins 217
Tyson, Mike 440

U

UEFA European Championship : 1992 victory by
Denmark 73; 2004 England defeat by France 489
Underarm bowling controversy in cricket 40, 332
Underwood, Derek 304
Underwood, Rory 416
University Boat Race : origin 133; Hugh Laurie 134
US Open (tennis) 264

V

van Barneveld, Raymond 110
van Basten, Marco 480
van Vuuren, Rudi 104
Vaughan, Michael 29
Velux 5 Oceans Race 27
Vendee Globe 27
Vialli, Gianluca 345
Vick, Michael 172

W

Wimbledon (tennis) : inaugural tournament 140; sisters in final 140; married female champion 141; name 159; qualifying tournament 229; trophies 264

Windsurfing 415

Wingfield, Walter Clopton 139

Wolf, Wolfgang 260

Wolfsburg 261

Woods, Tiger : career grand slam 7; name 8; world number 1 69; Masters Tournament Champions Dinner 189; PGA Grand Slam of Golf 283; strategy at 2006 Open Championship 401; Tiger Slam 404

Woodward, Clive 28

Woolmer, Bob : rebel tour to South Africa 304; death 305

Woosnam, Ian : PGA Grand Slam of Golf 283; Masters Tournament victory 284

Woosnam, Max : all round sportsman 104; England football captain 430

Wordsworth, Charles 133

Wordsworth, William 133

World Ice Golf Championships 473

World in Motion 268

World Series : Boston Red Sox record and 2004 comeback 9 ; Black Sox Scandal 10; New York Mets and New York Yankees victories 302; format and name 302

World Snooker Championship : overseas winners 25; Black Ball Final 240; maximum breaks 242

Wozniacki, Caroline : Rory McIlroy 466; world number 1 467

Wright, Billy 478

Wright, Ian 314

X

Y

Z

18447516R00099

Printed in Great Britain
by Amazon